The HORSEBACK Almanac

Jessica Jahiel, Ph.D.
Illustrations by Susan Spellman

ROXBURY PARK

LOWELL HOUSE

LOS ANGELES

CONTEMPORARY BOOKS

CHICAGO

Lowell House
2020 Avenue of the Stars, Suite 300
Los Angeles, CA 90067

Lowell House books can be purchased at special discounts when
ordered in bulk for premiums and special sales.
Contact Department TC at the above address.

Publisher: Jack Artenstein
Editor in Chief, Roxbury Park Books: Michael Artenstein
Director of Publishing Services: Rena Copperman
Managing Editor: Lindsey Hay
Designer: Shellie Pomeroy
Illustrations by: Susan Spellman

Jahiel, Jessica.
    The Horseback Almanac / Jessica Jahiel.
        p.   cm.
    Includes bibliographical references and index.
    Summary: An introduction to horseback riding, covering riding
        lessons, grooming, saddles and bridles, horse shows, riding groups,
        and more.
    ISBN 1-56565-952-X
    1. Horsemanship—Juvenile literature.   [1. Horsemanship.]
    I. Title.
    SF309.2.J34   1998
    798.2'3—dc21   97-38714
                                                        CIP
                                                        AC

Manufactured in the United States of America
10 9 8 7 6 5 4 3 2 1

This book is dedicated to my parents, who were my first, best examples of what teachers can be, and to all of my riding teachers, including the horses that taught me so much.

–J.J.

ACKNOWLEDGMENTS

Teaching children riding is one thing; teaching them horsemanship is quite another. I have the honor to be associated with two organizations that promote good horsemanship as well as good riding, and that are equally concerned with the safety and welfare of horses and riders.

To the American Riding Instructor Certification Program, which allows parents to find competent, safety-oriented instruction for their children—and for themselves!

To the United States Pony Clubs, Inc., which helps children to move up through a well-organized rating system as they improve their riding, their general knowledge, their horse management skills, and their horsemanship.

It has also been my pleasue to work with a number of riding instructors who are exceptional teachers of children: this group includes Ruth Ring Harvie, Hollyn Mangione, Juli McCarter, and Sue Brown. With their students as tomorrow's teachers, tomorrow's children will be in good hands.

CONTENTS

CHAPTER 1

GETTING STARTED

Do you love horses? Would you like to learn more about these beautiful animals? Even if you live in the city, you can find a way to enjoy horses. Trail rides, carriage rides, equestrian shows—there are a lot of different ways to spend time with and around horses.

If you want to be more personally involved with horses, you may want to learn to ride—and that means lessons. But before you proceed any further, you'll need to talk this over with your parents. They may be concerned about the expenses involved or may fear that riding is too dangerous. Riding lessons, as you will learn in chapter 3, are not much more expensive than swimming, tennis, skating, dance, or karate lessons. Riding schools usually provide their riders with equipment such as saddles, bridles, and helmets to use during lessons, so there is no obligation to purchase these things yourself. And, of course, you don't need to buy a horse! Riding schools have their own horses that they use for lessons.

A good riding school will have rules and regulations that promote the safety of the horses and riders. Required and recommended clothing

Do your parents think you're too young to ride? Send a stamped, self-addressed envelope for these FREE publications:

"When Can My Child Ride a Horse?" Write to: American Medical Equestrian Association, 103 Surry Road, Waynesville, NC 28786

"A Smart Start to Riding" Write to: American Horse Shows Association, 220 E. 42nd Street, New York, NY 10017

such as a helmet, boots, and gloves are designed with your safety in mind. And, of course, your parents are free to watch your lessons at any time.

The rewards of horseback riding are immeasurable. Riding is all teamwork and lets you build a special relationship with your partner: your horse. In most sports, you show up, play, and go home. Riding is different. You have a responsibility to the horse. You will learn how to groom and prepare your horse for each lesson, and you will learn how to take care of your horse after your ride. In horseback riding, you and your horse are dependent on each other; you must trust each other and work together as a team. In learning to ride, handle, and care for horses, you will develop a sense of responsibility and commitment that will carry into all other areas of your life. Whether you choose to ride for fun or competition, your love of riding will never fade. Not only will you learn to master the physically demanding challenges of riding, you will also develop an understanding and love of horses that will last a lifetime.

Let's begin by discussing the different types of riding.

English riding is the kind of riding that came to us from England. It's actually several different kinds of riding, but they are all basically alike. English riding is *sport* riding, which means it's just for fun, unlike Western riding, which began as a way to *work* from horseback. Western cowboys herded cattle, directing them from their home ranch to the market or the railway, which was sometimes several states away. Since the majority of sport and competitive riding is English, that will be the focus of this book.

In the United States, the most common forms of English riding are huntseat, show jumping, dressage, and eventing.

Huntseat riding, or "hunter riding," is based on the old English sport of foxhunting. In America, we also have an old foxhunting tradition, but most of today's "hunters" do their jumping in a showring, where they compete to see who can look the most elegant and jump the most neatly and smoothly.

Huntseat riding

Show jumping is faster, higher, and rougher. This is the exciting sport most often seen on television and in the Olympics. Riders on energetic, explosive horses compete over complicated courses of enormous jumps (fences), battling against each other and against the clock. If several horses get "clear rounds"—in other words, leave all the jumps standing—those horses will compete against each other in a fast "jump-off." The fastest and most agile horse will win.

Dressage, in contrast to the excitement of show jumping, is all polish and rhythm and quiet elegance. Dressage is both a system of training and a tradition of competing. The goal is the development and training of the horse so that it can perform difficult, complex movements easily, and respond to tiny, almost invisible signals from the rider. Dressage horses, like show jumpers, compete one at a time, alone in a marked arena. Each horse is judged on how well it performs its dressage test—a pattern of gaits, figures, and movements. At the very lowest levels, dressage tests consist of nothing more than walking and trotting. At the highest levels, the tests are complex and difficult, and the horses are truly spectacular. Dressage is for everyone—no matter whether you are a beginning rider or an expert, there's a competition at your level.

Eventing, also called "combined training," is the complete test of horse and rider. Eventing is a three-phase competition that combines the precision and rhythm of dressage with the courage and accuracy of show jumping—and then adds a third element, the cross-country phase. During this phase of competition, each horse and rider combination negotiates several miles of natural terrain, including water obstacles, ditches, and many man-made jumps. Sound scary? It doesn't have to be. Eventing, like dressage, is for everyone—again, no matter whether you are a beginner or an expert, you can find a competition at your level. You can start small and learn about eventing while you go "low and slow." Some beginner eventing competitions have walk-trot dressage tests and use poles on the ground, or even chalk marks, to serve as jumps for the cross-country and show-jumping phases.

There are a lot of different choices for horse lovers: trail riding, gymkhana (games on horseback), jumping, dressage, and eventing. But no matter which activity you prefer, all of them will begin the same way: You must choose a stable and instructor and begin taking lessons. Your first lessons will give you basic information about horses, grooming, and tack, and then you will begin to learn basic riding skills. But the most important part of lessons is learning from the right instructor, at a stable you enjoy.

CHAPTER 2

FINDING THE RIGHT STABLE AND INSTRUCTOR

WHAT TO LOOK FOR IN A STABLE

If you have never ridden before, you can start by looking in your telephone book. You'll find telephone numbers and addresses for stables and riding academies in the yellow pages. Make a list of these, and then call the ones that seem the most interesting. Your parents will appreciate it if you begin by calling the stables that are nearest to your home.

When you talk to the stable owners, find out what kind of riding they teach and what kind of program they offer to beginner riders. Many stables offer a lesson package of eight or ten lessons. If it sounds like fun, ask when you can come out and watch the instructor teaching a lesson to kids who are about your age.

When you visit the stable, here are some things for you and your parents to check:

- Is there a rule that all riders must wear ASTM/SEI protective helmets and safe footgear? If not, go look at another stable!

- Does the barn look clean and well organized? Are the stalls clean?

- Is the instructor calm and friendly, and focused on the riders in the lesson?

- Does the instructor speak clearly and make sense? Do the riders seem to understand the instructor?

- Are the riders having fun? Do they seem to be learning new things?

- Are the horses clean and shiny? Is the tack (equipment) clean and shiny?

- Are the horses quiet and under control?

- Are the students supposed to groom and tack up their horses for lessons? Do they learn these skills in the first few lessons?

- What kind of insurance does the barn carry? (Your parents will want to know whether the barn has a liability insurance policy.)

This may seem like a lot of questions to ask, but you need to know the answers. You want to be certain that you take lessons at a safe, well-run stable where the horses are treated well and the riders can learn and have fun safely.

HANDICAPPED RIDERS

If you love horses and are handicapped, don't be discouraged—you can still learn to ride. There are many programs designed especially for handicapped riders of all ages, and many stables have special equipment and specially trained horses, instructors, and assistants. There may be a program near you, so if an ordinary riding stable and lesson program don't meet your needs, don't give up! Contact the North American Riding for the Handicapped Association (NARHA) at (800) 369-7433, and find a way to put horses in your life.

CHOOSING AN INSTRUCTOR

Riding instructors are usually attached to stables. When you find a stable you like, it may have one resident instructor, or if it is a big stable, you may have your choice of several different instructors. They may all be equally good, but in case you aren't sure, and in case your parents want more objective criteria before you choose your instructor, there are particular things you should look for.

It isn't always easy to find a good riding instructor. In the United States, anyone can claim to be a riding teacher—there are no national regulations, requirements, or exams. But it's very important for you to find a competent, safety-oriented instructor who can teach you to ride well. How can you tell?

One good way to begin your search is to look for a certified instructor. Some instructors take their jobs very seriously and voluntarily take certification exams to prove that they are competent teachers, know good horsemanship, and are safety-oriented. Look for an instructor who is certified by the American Riding Instructor Certification Program (ARICP). If your instructor is ARICP-certified, he or she is a good bet.

There are some other programs that certify riding instructors. If you can't find an ARICP instructor, look for one who has certification from the Camp Horsemanship Association (CHA) or from the Horsemanship Safety Association (HSA). If your instructor is from England, he or she should be certified by the British Horse Society (BHS), or by the Canadian Equestrian Federation (CEF) if from Canada.

Certification is very important, but there are other things to look for too. Some important qualities, like attitude, don't show up on exams. Look for an instructor who is cheerful and positive, patient and kind, and who recognizes what you *can* do and then helps you prepare for the things that you can't do yet. Look for an instructor who really loves the horses and who speaks up for them—someone who won't let students kick the horses or pull the reins too hard. Look for an instructor who *explains* things so that you can understand them and who doesn't mind explaining something several times, in several different ways, until it makes sense to you.

Here are some signs of a good instructor:

- The horses look cheerful and healthy.

- The other students look happy and seem to be learning.

- You can understand the instructor's explanations and instructions.

- You are excited when you are asked to do something new, because you feel that you are ready for it.

- You learn horsemanship along with riding skills.

Here are some signs of a bad instructor:

- The horses look unhappy and unhealthy.

- The other students seem upset, nervous, frightened, or bored, and don't appear to be learning much.

- Nothing is explained or you don't understand the explanations.

- You feel frightened when you are asked to do something new, because you don't feel prepared.

Take your time, look carefully, and find the very best instructor you can, because a good instructor will look after your safety and help you get the very most out of your lessons.

Chapter 3

YOUR RIDING LESSONS

Riding lessons can be group, semiprivate, or private lessons. Which one is best for you?

GROUP OR PRIVATE?

Private lessons are best for beginners and for advanced riders, who need the most focused individual attention.

Your very first lessons should be private, because everything will be new, your instructor will have a lot to tell and show you, and you will have a lot of questions. Later on, especially when you are comfortable cantering and jumping, you may enjoy sharing a semiprivate lesson with one other rider or a group lesson with two or three other riders.

Intermediate riders can benefit from watching each other and participating in group activities, while beginners and advanced riders usually benefit most from private lessons. But whatever sort of lessons you take, private or group, what matters most is that you are safe and have fun while you learn to ride.

THE COST OF LESSONS

Assuming that you'll be signing up for one-hour sessions, lessons will cost anywhere from $15 or $20 if you are one rider among three or four in a group lesson, to $30 or $40 for a lesson shared with one other rider, up to $50 or $75 if you get individual instruction from a well-known riding instructor. This may seem like a lot, but remember that the instructor is dealing with *two* live beings—you *and* the horse—and these costs aren't very different from the amount you are probably already paying for dance, music, skating, swimming, or tennis lessons. Some stables and some instructors will offer a discount on a paid-in-advance package of ten or twelve lessons. If you are sure that you've found the right instructor for you, this might be a good idea.

WHAT TO WEAR

Riding clothes may look fancy or awkward, but they are really based on what is practical, comfortable, and safe for the sport. The more you know about riding, the more sensible riding clothes will seem.

Safety Gear: Helmets and Boots

Your instructor and the riding stable will almost certainly insist that you wear an ASTM/SEI-approved riding helmet. If they don't insist on it, find another stable where safety is a priority! Safety should be any riding stable's *first* concern. Eventually, you will want to have a helmet of your own. It's an excellent investment in your safety, and it's the first piece of equipment you should buy. Helmets come in many shapes, sizes, and styles, and in a large

The traditional helmet can be protected by a colorful nylon/lycra cover, or by a black cover for show riding.

variety of colors and patterns, so you should have no trouble finding one that looks good and fits you perfectly.

Your helmet must have a label that says ASTM/SEI—that's how you know it meets national safety standards. Different brands fit differently, so try on many helmets until you find the one that fits you best and is most comfortable when it is on and fastened. When you try on your helmet, be sure that your hair is the way it will be when you ride. Helmets fit differently over braids and ponytails. When your helmet is on your head, move it up and down—it should be snug enough to wriggle your eyebrows up and down, but not so tight that it hurts.

Keep the helmet on and the chin strap, or harness, fastened whenever you are on a horse. You should wear your safety helmet, properly fastened, every time you ride, and it's an even better idea to put the helmet on when you get to the barn and take it off just before you go home. The new helmets are light, comfortable and cool, and will add to your safety without getting in your way. Always wait until you dismount before you undo your chin strap.

If you ever have a fall and hit your

Jewelry and Safety

Jewelry and riding don't mix well, so plan to leave your jewelry at home when you go to your riding lessons. Rings can pinch your fingers; necklaces can catch on the harness of your safety helmet; and bracelets can catch on the girth buckles when you are tacking up, and on the reins and the horse's mane when you are riding. Leave the jewelry at home! Many riders have pierced ears, but even earrings can be trouble—they can catch on the harness of your helmet, or in your own hair. If you must wear earrings, be sure to wear tiny studs, never hoops or dangles.

head, the helmet should be sent back to the manufacturer for inspection, and replacement if necessary. The damage is to the interior; it's not something you can see by looking at the outside or the inside of the helmet. Many helmet manufacturers offer a big discount on replacement helmets, so replacing a damaged helmet won't cost as much as buying a new one. But even if it did, it would be worth it.

paddock boots

tall riding boots

After the safety helmet, safe footgear must be your second priority. Sandals, ordinary sneakers, jellies, and running shoes are not safe for riding. Riding boots, paddock boots, and special riding sneakers are designed for riding safety, with a small heel and a one-piece sole. The heel keeps your leg from sliding completely through the stirrup, and the one-piece sole lets your foot slide out of the stirrup quickly if you fall. You may like the look of the tall black riding boots, but good ones are usually very expensive and cheap ones are usually very uncomfortable. Tall boots are appropriate for older riders whose bodies have achieved full growth. Don't buy expensive riding boots while you are still growing! Even the most expensive custom-made boots won't fit well or be comfortable for very long if you are busy outgrowing them. Instead, look for good paddock boots, which will come up just over your ankles, or for the new riding sneakers, which are designed for walking comfort and riding safety, and come in low-cut or high-top styles and in many colors.

Helmets and boots don't have to be expensive items. Some approved helmets cost as little as $45, and you may already have a pair of shoes or boots in your closet that will do nicely for your first few lessons. Your riding instructor will be able to advise you about appro-

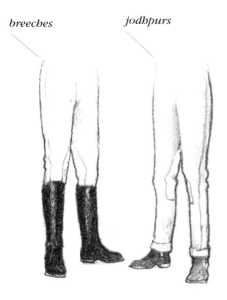

breeches   jodhpurs

Riding pants

priate footgear and may even be able to tell you where you can buy the kind of boots you want at the best price.

Riding Pants

You may be comfortable riding in your jeans, or in riding tights or leggings. If not, ask your riding instructor to recommend a source for inexpensive jodhpurs. Boots and breeches (the type of riding pants worn with tall boots) look pretty, but they are meant for older riders whose legs and feet have finished growing. If you desperately want breeches and tall boots, check the barn bulletin boards for items that someone else may have outgrown. You should also keep an eye on your local tack shop; many shops have a few pairs of secondhand boots for sale at low prices. Otherwise, look for short boots and jodhpurs, which are riding pants that extend all the way down to your ankles. If you wear riding sneakers or low paddock boots, be careful not to accidentally buy breeches in place of jodhpurs. If you do, you'll have an uncomfortable gap between the top of your short boots and the bottom of your breeches.

Shirts

Unless your riding program requires a special kind of shirt, just be sensible—T-shirts, polo shirts, and sweatshirts can all be perfectly appropriate and very comfortable riding attire. Ask your instructor if he or she has a preference, and find out whether the stable sells

Catalogs

Miller's Harness Shop
1-800-553-7655

Dover Saddlery
1-800-989-1500

Stateline Tack
1-800-228-9208

Tack in the Box
1-800-456-8225

Whip 'n Spur Tack Shop
1-800-944-7677

Hartmeyer Saddlery
1-800-225-5519

Beval Saddlery
1-800-524-0136

Libertyville Saddle Shop
1-800-871-3353

T-shirts with the stable name on them. Sometimes many stables share the same grounds, and it's fun to wear a T-shirt that identifies your stable. Try to avoid wearing oversize, long, loose T-shirts, oversize sweatshirts, or loose shirts with the tails hanging out. Wearing a shirt that fits reasonably well and tucking it in whenever you ride will make it much easier for your riding instructor to evaluate your position and help you improve it. It's also a good idea because it will keep you safe—and discreet. A too-long, too-loose shirt can catch on the saddle when you dismount, and you can end up with your shirt over your head!

Gloves

If the reins hurt your fingers, or if you have nice fingernails that you want to keep clean and unbroken, you will want to wear gloves when you ride. You will

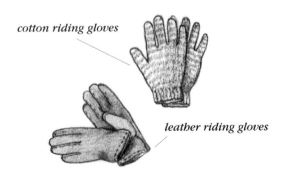

cotton riding gloves

leather riding gloves

find many types of riding gloves at your local tack shop. Riding gloves are designed for riding, and they have reinforcements where your hands hold the reins: between the fourth and little finger, and between the thumb and first finger. Simple cotton gloves with pimpled rubber grips along the fingers are inexpensive, cool, and very useful. Gloves with crocheted string backs and leather palms are strong, cool and comfortable. Be sure to try on the gloves and check that the fingers are long enough for you. When you ride, your fingers will need to be closed on the reins, which can be hard to manage if your gloves are too tight or the fingers are too short.

Riding equipment and clothing catalogs are not just informative—they can also be a lot of fun to look through, and very helpful when someone asks you what you want for your birthday! Whenever you visit a tack shop, ask if they have a catalog that you can take home, and also put your name on their mailing list. Looking through tack and clothing catalogs is a great way to become familiar with the names, styles, and purpose of clothing, saddles, bridles, and other equipment.

WHAT TO EXPECT FROM LESSONS

You should expect to have fun, you should expect to be reasonably safe, and you should expect to learn something. If any of these three factors is missing, then the instructor you've chosen may not be the one for you.

You should expect to *participate* in your lesson! That means listening to your instructor and making an effort to do what you are asked to do. Try to understand what he or she is saying, and if you don't understand, *ask*. It's your instructor's job to teach you, yes—but it's *your* job to *learn*. And you know perfectly well that nobody, not even the best teacher in the world, can teach you anything at all unless you *want* to learn (remember those flute lessons?).

In your first year of riding lessons, you should be able to learn how to ride comfortably and securely at a walk, trot, and canter; how to stop, start, and turn your horse; and how to increase and decrease your horse's speed at each gait. Your first few months of lessons will probably be private lessons, always on the same horse. As you learn more and as your riding improves, you will have lessons on different horses and learn to share the arena with others in a lesson.

A good instructor will be organized and will have a plan for your lessons so that you will learn in a building-block fashion, with each lesson adding to and building on the previous one.

You should expect to go away from every lesson knowing a little bit more about horses and riding than you did when you got to the stable. You should *not* expect too much; no riding instructor is going to make you an expert rider in ten lessons, just as no tennis instructor can make you ready for Wimbledon in ten lessons. Some riders can learn to post the trot, for example, in their first five lessons. Some learn on their tenth lesson, and others on their twentieth! Different people learn different skills at different rates, and not every rider has the exact same abilities and talents. That's normal. The important thing to ask yourself after every lesson is *not* "Did I catch up with Jane?" but "Did I learn something today? Did I have fun? Do I feel good about myself and my sport?"

A good instructor will teach you much more than how to ride; you should also learn about horses: horse nature, horse handling, and horse care.

Chapter 4

ABOUT HORSES

BREEDS

There are hundreds of different horse breeds in the world. Here are some of the most popular breeds in the United States. All of them are very suitable for English riding, as they are strong, intelligent, smooth, and versatile.

- Arabian: the oldest recognized pure breed; relatively small, sensitive, affectionate; suitable for capable, sensitive riders. Arabians make wonderful horses for endurance riding and competitive trail rides.

- Thoroughbred: the ultimate racing breed; sensitive and fast; suitable for capable, sensitive riders. Thoroughbreds excel at hunting, jumping, and polo.

- Quarter Horse: combines speed, agility, great strength, and a calm, pleasant, nature. Quarter Horses make excellent family horses.

- Appaloosa: strong, extremely versatile spotted horses that often resemble Thoroughbreds or Quarter Horses in body type.

- Morgan: small, agile, energetic; a versatile athlete. Morgans are very popular as police horses and carriage horses.

- Saddlebred: beautiful, flashy, elegant. The Saddlebred is another American breed with a sweet temperament.

- Standardbred: when their harness-racing careers are over, Standardbreds make wonderful, good-tempered, gentle riding horses.

- Crossbred: these horses are combinations of two breeds. Some crossbreeds are so popular that they eventually become a recognized breed, like the Morab (Morgan + Arabian) or Anglo-Arab (Arabian + Thoroughbred).

COLORS

- Bay: the body color will range from bright red to reddish-brown. A bay horse always has black "points": The mane, tail, and lower legs will be black.

- Chestnut: the body color will range from yellow red to a deep reddish brown, with a matching or lighter mane and tail. Occasionally, a chestnut horse will have a flaxen mane and tail, a mixture of white, brown, and black hairs, which appears mostly straw-colored. A chestnut horse's mane and tail will *never* be black.

- Palomino: golden horse with white mane and tail.

- Buckskin: beige or tan body with black points.

- Gray: a mixture of black and white hairs; the proportion of black to white changes over time. Young gray horses may look dark gray or dappled, but as they age, each new coat is a little lighter. An old gray horse can actually look pure white.

- Roan: a mixture of white and colored hairs. The colors do not change as the horse ages.

A Horse of a Different Color

Good horses come in all colors, but when you are learning to ride, there is only one important color to avoid: green. A "green" horse is young or un-schooled. A "green" rider is a person who is just learning how to ride. Green horses do best with experi-enced riders who can look after them and teach them, and green riders do best with experienced school horses. A green rider-green horse combination will get into trouble, and that's why a horseman's least favorite color combination is green-on-green!

27

A gray's coat will become lighter with time, whereas a roan's will not.

- Red roan: a mixture of chestnut and white, which can look reddish-pink.

- Blue roan: a mixture of black and white, which can look like a very dark gray.

- Black: horse with black hair and black skin. Black horses can be difficult to tell from dark brown horses, but if you see brown hairs in a horse's muzzle and flank, the horse is brown.

- Pinto: horse with a coat of two or more colors. A black-and-white pinto is called a piebald, and a brown-and-white pinto is called a skewbald.

MARKINGS

White markings on the horse's face and lower legs can occur with any body color.

star   *snip*   *strip*

Facial markings

- Star: white mark on the horse's forehead

- Snip: white mark on the horse's nose

- Strip: narrow white stripe down the center of the horse's face

- Blaze: wide white stripe down the center of the horse's face

- Bald face: face that is entirely white

Leg markings

- Coronets: white just above the hoof

- Socks: white from the hoof partway up the horse's ankle and lower leg

- Stockings: white extending from the hoof farther up the horse's lower leg, toward the knee

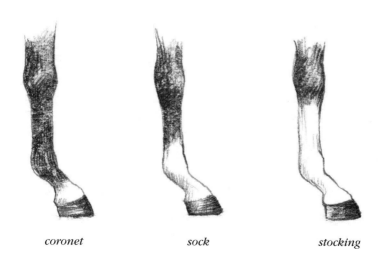

coronet   *sock*   *stocking*

Gaited Horses

Some horses have other gaits besides the walk, trot, canter, and gallop. Tennessee Walking Horses, American Saddlebreds, Missouri Fox Trotters, Peruvian Pasos, Paso Finos, and Icelandic Horses are all "gaited"; in other words, they have special ways of moving. Gaited horses can be very smooth and pleasant to ride.

On a horse's registration papers, there are silhouettes of horses with markings drawn in to match the horse's actual markings. So many horses could be described in general terms, such as "star and one white foot," that it's important to be very precise when you list a horse's markings. The above-described horse could be one of many, but it would be easier to identify if the description were "few white hairs in forehead just above and between eyes; white half-coronet."

GAITS

Walk

The walk is a relaxed, four-beat gait. It's the easiest gait for beginner riders, because it is gentle and slow. It is also the gait that any rider will use during the first part of a ride, to help the horse warm up and stretch before the real work begins.

Trot

The trot is a faster, more powerful gait than the walk. The trot is a two-beat gait. At the trot, a horse moves its legs in diagonal pairs: from one front leg and the opposite hind leg, to the other front leg and its opposite hind leg. The trot has more "push" from behind than the walk, and the rider will feel much more movement. A thoughtful rider will trot his or her horse only after having walked it to warm it up, and the rider won't canter until he or she has trotted.

Canter

The canter is smoother and easier to ride than the trot, but it is a more complicated gait than the walk or trot. It's a three-beat gait that has a rhythm of *one-two-three-pause, one-two-three-pause*. The *one-two-three* beats are the horse's legs touching the ground, and the pause comes when the horse has all four legs in the air for an instant. If you watch carefully when a horse canters, you'll see the pattern: One hind leg touches the ground, digs in, and pushes the horse's body forward. Next, the other hind leg and the opposite front leg touch the ground together. Then the other front leg touches the ground, after which all four legs are *off* the ground! That sequence is *one* canter stride. Then one hind leg touches the ground, and the next stride begins.

Horses move straight at a walk and trot, but at the canter, they are curved a little. A horse cantering is a little like a person skipping; it moves forward but also moves a little bit sideways. When you skip, one of your legs moves a little ahead of the other—the same thing happens when a horse canters. The front leg on one side reaches a little ahead of the other front leg. This leg is called the leading leg, and if it's the left front leg, the horse is on the left lead. If it's the right front leg, the horse is on the right lead. Riders prefer their horses to use the lead that matches the direction they are going. For instance, they would prefer the right lead when going around the arena to the right (the right side of the horse and rider faces the inside of the arena), and the left lead when going to the left. The little bend in the horse's body matches the direction, and this makes the horse better balanced and more comfortable.

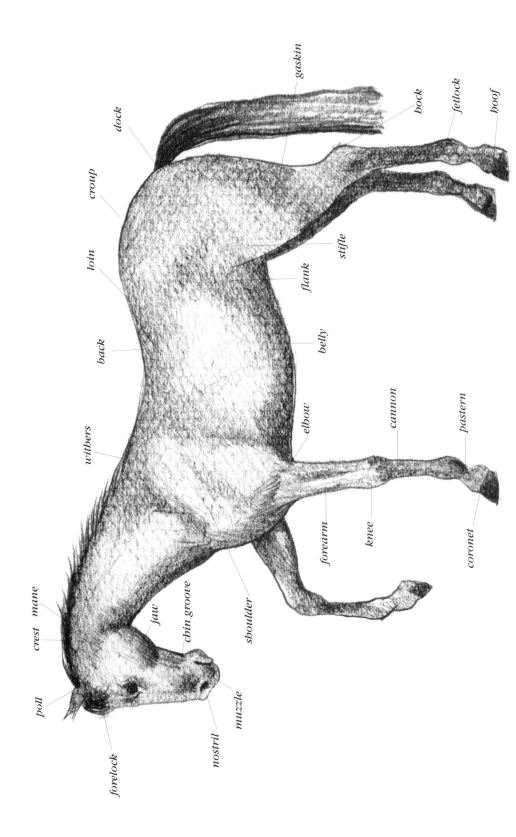

gaskin

dock

hock

fetlock

hoof

croup

loin

stifle

flank

back

belly

withers

elbow

cannon

pastern

crest mane

jaw

chin groove

forearm

knee

poll

shoulder

coronet

forelock

nostril

muzzle

HORSES' BASIC NATURE

To be safe around horses, you need to understand their nature. Horses have certain basic reactions that are always present, no matter how calm, old, or well trained an individual horse may be.

Whenever you are around horses, there are two key words you should remember: *quiet* and *slow.* Speak quietly around horses—never yell or scream. Move slowly around horses—never jump, run, or make sudden movements.

Horses and even ponies are bigger than humans, but they are nervous and sensitive animals with very quick reactions. Loud noises and sudden movements scare them, and frightened horses can react by running away, jerking back, kicking, or biting.

If your movements and your voice are always quiet, calm, and friendly, your horse will see you as a friend.

"READING" HORSES

Horses have very expressive faces and very clear body language. If you pay attention, you will know whether a horse is comfortable or uncomfortable, feeling relaxed and secure, or feeling tense and nervous.

Sensitivity

Your horse's sense of hearing and sense of smell are much, much more sensitive than yours. This can add to your fun on trail rides! If you pay close attention to your horse and its reactions, you may see all sorts of things that you might otherwise miss. Look where your horse is looking, and you may see birds, deer, hunters in camouflage outfits, or other horses far away.

You can tell a lot about how your horse is feeling and what it is thinking from watching it. Checking out its eyes and ears, tail, muscles, and movement is a good way to find out what is on your horse's mind.

Eyes

Eyes wide open with whites showing mean the horse is frightened. There is an exception to this: Some Appaloosas have eyes that show the white edges all the time, so with these horses you would need to read other features such as ears and posture.

Eyes half-shut means the horse is relaxed and sleepy. You'll see this when you are giving your horse a good grooming or when you scratch an itchy spot on its neck.

Ears

Ears pointing forward means the horse is looking ahead, in the direction that its ears are pointing. If its ears are stiff and unmoving, the horse is completely focused on whatever is in front of it, and is either frightened or about to become frightened.

Ears pointing flat back along the horse's neck means the horse is angry and warning whoever is there (such as another horse, a human, or a dog) that it is seriously thinking about kicking or biting.

This horse's eyes, looking straight ahead, and its ears, slightly uneven, reveal that it is relaxed and attentive.

Ears uneven—one forward, one back, or both ears swiveling gently—means the horse is paying attention to its rider (if it has one) and to its surroundings. The horse isn't frightened or worried, just attentive.

Tail

You won't be able to see your horse's tail when you're riding him, but you can watch other horses to see what they do with their tails.

A relaxed, comfortable horse at rest will have a tail that hangs straight down. When the horse is moving, the tail will be carried away from its body and will swing gently from side to side.

A tense horse will sometimes clamp its tail tightly to its body.

An excited horse running and playing will carry its tail high, sometimes so high that it looks like a flag.

A tail that goes around in circles is the

A relaxed horse will allow its tail to hang straight down.

sign of an anxious, unhappy horse. When you see a horse wringing its tail, try to figure out what is causing this problem.

Muscles

A relaxed horse standing in the sun, head hanging and eyes half-shut, will feel soft to the touch, with no tension anywhere. The neck muscles will feel particularly soft.

Hard muscles, especially in the neck, means a horse is frightened and tense; all of its big muscles seem hard and rigid. Patting the neck of a tense horse feels like patting a rock!

Did You Know . . .

Horses are measured in "hands." A hand is four inches, so a horse that is 14.3 hands would be 59 inches tall (14 x 4 inches = 56 inches, plus 3 inches = 59 inches). Horses are measured from the ground to the withers, which is the part just in front of the saddle, before the neck begins. The hand probably began as the average width of a man's hand and then, over the years, became standardized at four inches.

Movement

A comfortable, secure horse, even if it has a lot of energy, will be balanced and light on its feet. When it canters around the field or arena, there won't be a lot of noise from its hooves. A tense, uncomfortable, or worried horse will be less balanced and much less light on its feet. One worried horse cantering can make enough noise for a whole group of horses.

A bored horse—for instance, an old school horse that spends most of each day carrying beginner riders in an arena—will often use just enough energy to stay out of trouble. If a healthy horse shuffles its feet and lumps along with its nose on the ground, the horse is probably very bored indeed. Bored horses can perk up and become almost unrecognizable if you take them out of the stable and ride them on trails.

Horses don't like to be bullied, but they like to have someone in charge. That "someone" can be you! Horses will accept your signals and try to do what you ask them to do, as long as they are not frightened or hurt. Horses appreciate kind treatment and soft voices, and if you treat them kindly and fairly, and talk to them softly, they will respond with appreciation. The way horses react to you will depend on the way you approach and handle them, and on your ability to understand what their body language is telling you.

BASIC EQUIPMENT: HALTER AND LEAD ROPE

When you learn to handle horses at your riding stable, the first pieces of equipment you will use are a halter and lead rope. When you take your horse out of its stall or field, you will need to put the halter on its head and lead it by the lead rope. Never try to lead a horse with only a halter!

When you approach a horse, speak to it so that it knows you are there. Don't approach it directly from the front or stand immediately in front of it or try to touch it on the front of its face. Real horsepeople don't ever pet a strange horse on the face. They always approach from the side and stroke it on the neck. Horses can see all around them quite well, but there are two places they cannot see you coming from:

Putting on a halter (with leadrope around horse's neck)

directly behind them and directly in front of them. Always approach a horse from the left side. Move toward its neck and shoulder, stroke it on the neck or shoulder, and talk to it.

To put the halter on the horse, first take the end of the lead rope in your left hand and reach your right arm over its neck. Take the end of the lead rope in your hand and pull it around its neck. This gives you something to hold while you put the halter on the horse. Take the unbuckled halter crownpiece in your left hand and reach for it over the horse's neck with your right hand, just as you reached for the rope. Hold the rope and the halter crownpiece in your right hand, and bring the halter noseband over the horse's nose with your left hand. Then slide your left hand up the halter cheekpiece until you reach the buckle, and fasten the crownpiece to the buckle. Now you can take the lead rope off the horse's neck and use it to lead him away.

Keep a double grip on the lead rope, with your right hand about twelve inches under the horse's chin, and your left hand holding the rest of the rope. The double grip will allow you to hold onto the horse with your left hand if it startles and jerks the rope from your right hand. If the rope is long, fold the extra length back and forth, and hold the folds. Never, under *any* circumstances, wrap a lead rope or a longe line or a bridle rein or anything else around your hand. If the horse jumps, spooks, or runs away, you can get caught, dragged, and badly hurt. Even a brief jump or a sudden startle can break a finger or wrist if there's a lead rope or rein wrapped around it. This is important: Whatever you are holding—lead rope, longe line, rein, or haystring—if there is a horse at the other end of it, *don't wrap it around your hand.*

LEADING A HORSE

When you lead a horse, its head should be near your shoulder. If the horse's head is in front of you or behind you, you have much less control. When you are in position, standing next to the horse and looking forward, step out energetically and speak to the horse at the same time. Use its name and tell it to "walk" or "walk on." Don't look at the horse—look ahead toward where you are going, and your horse will be much more likely to go with you.

If the horse is reluctant to move forward, don't turn around and try to pull it forward. It won't work! Instead, take the horse sideways at first, so that you are actually pushing instead of pulling it. One or two steps to the right or left will usually "unglue" a stuck horse.

When you put the horse back into its stall or field, take the halter off in the same way—putting the lead rope around its neck first, so that you can unbuckle the halter and remove it quietly before you remove the rope and let the horse go. Moving quietly and calmly, and giving the horse a small treat before you let it go and another small treat after you let it go, will encourage it to stand and let you walk away from it, instead of jerking away from you, kicking up its heels, and running off.

Halters should always be unbuckled

Giving a Horse a Treat

You know about apples, carrots, and sugar lumps, but did you know that horses also love raisins and dry pasta shells? The safest way to give your horse a treat is to put the food in its feeder. If you want to offer it a treat from your hand, be careful! Never offer your horse a treat by holding it in your fingers. Open your hand so that the palm is very flat, put the treat in your palm, and let the horse take it.

Tying a Quick-Release Knot

Your instructor will teach you how to tie a quick-release knot. This is the best knot to use when you tie a horse to anything solid, because you can undo the knot just by pulling on the loose end of the rope. An ordinary knot will get tighter and tighter, and harder and harder to loosen, if a horse pulls back against it.

before they are put on or taken off a horse's head. You may see other people who unclip the halter and push it onto the horse's head, over its ears, with the buckle still fastened, and later pull it off the horse's head, over its ears, with the buckle still fastened. This is lazy, unkind, and poor horsemanship. Horses have sensitive ears, and this can cause them to become "head-shy," which means that they will react badly to having their heads or ears touched. A head-shy horse can be very difficult to bridle.

Whenever you handle a horse, be clear, calm, and definite. Don't jump, run, yell, or do anything that could startle or frighten the horse. Never be violent or abrupt. But it's also important not to be tentative. Even if you are nervous, act as though you are quite sure of yourself. Horses are herd animals, and herds always have a pecking order. Whenever you are handling a horse, *one* of you has to be the leader. If you are clear and definite, the leader will be you. Hitting and yelling are *not* leader behaviors. They are bully behaviors, and the horse will not respond well to them. It will respond very well to quiet confidence, so that is what you want to display.

Your instructor will teach you other skills: how to tie and crosstie the horse, for example. You will need to know how to do this so that you will have both hands free to groom the horse. If the horse is wearing a halter, you will tie the horse by its lead rope, or attach the crossties to each side of the halter. If the horse is wearing a bridle and you need to tie it up temporarily, either remove the bridle and replace it with a halter, or put on the halter *over* the bridle. Never tie a horse by the bridle! The reins can break, and if the horse pulls back, it can damage its mouth. Put the reins over the horse's head, put the buckle in the middle of the saddle, and tuck the rein under the left stirrup. This will give the horse enough freedom to stretch its neck but won't let the reins slide down where it could step on them or get its feet tangled in them.

CHAPTER 5

GROOMING AND GROOMING EQUIPMENT

Horses need to be kept clean and comfortable, so riders groom their horses before they tack up. You will need to learn about grooming equipment—what to use and how to use it.

HOW AND WHY TO GROOM

Each horse will have its own grooming equipment, just the way you have your own toothbrush and washcloth. Your horse's grooming equipment will include a hoofpick; a stiff brush with long bristles called a dandy brush; a softer brush with shorter bristles, called a body brush; a rubber currycomb; a metal currycomb; and various rags and sponges. But even if your grooming kit consists of only a hoofpick, a rubber currycomb, and a dandy brush, you can do a good job of making your horse clean and comfortable.

First, before you do anything at all, be sure that your horse is safely tied or crosstied. Even if a horse is quiet and sweet and you trust it very much, don't try to groom the horse without tying it up. If the aisles are crowded and you need to groom a horse in its stall, that's fine—

you can tie it there. If the horse isn't tied, it will move around much more, and you will run the risk of getting stepped on. Horses can't see what is just next to or under their feet—even if what's under their feet is *you*!

If your horse is very dirty, you will need to start with the rubber currycomb, rubbing it all over the horse's neck and body in a circular motion in the direction of hair growth. This will loosen the dirt. A rubber currycomb isn't a harsh tool, but there are places where a horse is quite sensitive—on its face, on its lower legs, and over bony surfaces (knees, hocks, elbows, hips)—so be careful not to dig in too hard. You want the horse to enjoy being groomed.

metal currycomb

sponge

dandy brush

hoofpick

rubber currycomb

Grooming equipment

Next, you will take the dandy brush and, starting at the top of the neck, brush the loose dirt out of the horse's coat. Brush in short, deep, sharp strokes so that you are lifting the dirt up out of the horse's coat instead of just touching the surface of the hair (and leaving the dirt in place). As you brush, after every two or three strokes, rub the brush through the metal currycomb. This transfers the dirt to the currycomb, so that you don't keep brushing the same dirt into the horse. Metal currycombs are only for cleaning brushes and should never be used on the horse. If the horse is standing in a cement aisle or on rubber mats, you can tap the metal currycomb sharply on the floor whenever you've run the brush through it ten or fifteen times. This will keep the comb from filling up with dirt and transferring it back onto the brush. Take a look at the ground after you tap the currycomb. You'll see a neat pile of dust and dirt in the shape of the comb, and you'll know that you took all that dirt out of your horse's coat!

When the horse seems clean, brush it all over again with the body brush, again using the metal currycomb to keep the body brush clean. After this, your horse should have a visibly cleaner, shinier coat! If your grooming box includes stable cloths or rags, wipe the horse down with a damp cloth. If it includes sponges, you can wash out the horse's eyes and nose. Finally, use the hoofpick to clean out each of its hooves, one at a time.

Your instructor will show you how to pick up and hold your horse's feet. Lean into the horse and gently pinch the tendon at the back of the horse's lower leg. Use a verbal signal as well—most horses have been trained to respond to "foot" or "up" and will pick up the foot willingly. When you pick up your horse's feet to clean them, stay close to its body. This will make it easier for you to pick up its feet, and easier for the horse to hold them up and keep its balance. When your horse lifts its foot, quickly and gently cup the toe in your hand so that the

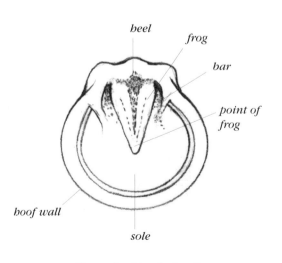

heel

frog

bar

point of frog

hoof wall

sole

The underside of a hoof

bottom of the horse's foot makes a flat surface in front of you. Then you can use the point of the hoofpick to clean the foot, scraping all dirt and rocks out of the crevices. The point of the hoofpick should move *away* from you—always clean the hooves from heel to toe. The crevices between the sole and frog (the triangular protrusion at the heel) are quite deep toward the heel, so be especially careful to get all dirt and pebbles out of this area. And while you are cleaning the hooves, notice if any of the horse's shoes are loose! If you find a loose one, bring it to your instructor's attention.

Grooming lets you learn about your horse—and it lets your horse learn about you. Horses enjoy a good scratchy grooming, and they like the people who make them feel good.

GROOMING SAFETY TIPS

The best overall safety tip applies to grooming, riding, and everything else you could ever do with, on, or around a horse: *Stay alert.* Notice your horse's movements and its mood, and what is going on around you. Even the kindest, quietest horse can become frightened or "spooked" and jump or kick.

Giving a Horse a Bath

If you spend a lot of time at the stable, you may get to give a hot, sweaty horse a bath. Here's what you will need:

- *A place to wash the horse (wash stall or wash rack)*
- *A source of water (hose or buckets)*
- *Horse shampoo*
- *A soft rubber currycomb or scrub brush*
- *A sweat scraper to remove the excess water from the horse*
- *A set of dry clothes for you to change into after the bath*

Keep the water away from the horse's face and ears, and use less shampoo than you think you need.

Scrub and rinse, rinse again, then rinse one more time than you think you should. You don't want to leave itchy shampoo in the horse's coat!

When the horse is clean, ask if you can take it for a walk and let it eat grass while its coat dries. Nothing feels softer or nicer than a clean, dry horse after a bath!

Part of being alert during grooming is noticing things about your horse's body. Notice which direction the hair grows on its neck, sides, and back, and always brush the hair in *that* direction. Your dog or cat would be unhappy if you stroked or brushed it against the direction of its hair growth. Your horse will be just as unhappy, and it's a lot larger!

Notice where your horse is itchy— most horses love to be scratched on the withers, as well as halfway up the neck, just below the mane. Every horse's itchy spots are in a slightly different place. If you learn where your horse's itchy spots are, you'll be able to scratch them whenever you groom it and whenever you want to reassure the horse or just make it feel good.

Also notice where your horse is ticklish! Most horses, like humans, are ticklish in some spots. With humans, the most ticklish areas are usually the sides, and the bottoms of the feet. With horses, the most ticklish areas are usually the area just behind the elbows, where the girth lies, and the flank, which is the concave area behind the ribcage and before the hindquarters. Since you have to brush both of these areas, be careful—sensitive horses sometimes kick if they are tickled in those spots. Don't skip those spots when you are grooming your horse, but don't touch them too lightly, either—that will make them tickle even more! Think of how your own ticklish areas feel. If the bottoms of your feet are ticklish, would you prefer having them touched very lightly or with some pressure? Your horse feels the same way! Instead of just barely touching those ticklish areas, brush them slowly and carefully, with some pressure on the brush. This turns a tickle into a scratch, and your horse will appreciate it.

While you groom your horse, you should also be alert for signs of discomfort. Grooming can help you notice if your horse is sore anywhere. Sore spots can cause a horse to react to a currycomb or brush by flinching away, dropping its back, or pinning its ears. If your horse begins reacting this way when you groom a particular spot, tell your instructor or the stable manager immediately so that they can find out what is wrong and take care of the horse.

If it's summer and the flies are biting, your horse may be shifting around, twisting its head, stamping, and even trying to bite at pesky flies. This can be dangerous to you! Be aware of the presence of biting flies, even if your jodhpurs, boots, and long-sleeved shirt are protecting you from the bites. If there is a fan in the grooming area, turning it on will often keep flies away from the horse. If not, put fly spray on your horse's legs and under its belly before you do any more grooming. Be sure to find out whether your horse minds being sprayed—some horses object to this very strenuously and need to have the liquid wiped on them instead. Flies are also very fond of horses' faces and ears. Don't spray around the horse's face and eyes; you'll need to put some fly spray on a rag and wipe it on those areas.

When you are grooming a horse's legs, you can bend your knees, lean down, bend over, or crouch—but never sit or kneel on the ground.

You must be able to move back, out of the horse's way, instantly.

When you groom a horse, you need to groom both sides. To do this, you may need to walk behind your horse while it is tied up for grooming. Speak to the horse, put one hand on its neck or side, move it back to the horse's rump, and move around behind it with your body very close to the horse's backside. If it kicks out in surprise, it could hurt you badly if you were at arm's length, but if you are right up against it, you will only get bumped. The reason for putting your hand on the horse's side first, then sliding it around to the rump, is that horses can startle and kick out when their rumps are touched suddenly.

When you groom your horse's head, stand a little to one side. When you hold a horse for someone else, stand a little to one side—never stand directly in front of a horse. This is an important safety precaution. A startled horse can jump forward, and a horse cannot see you if you are directly in front of its nose!

Remember that you should never stand directly in front of or directly behind a horse! When you pick up a front foot to clean it, stand by the horse's shoulder. When you pick up a hind foot, stand by the horse's hip. If you are brushing your horse's tail, do the same—stand beside the horse, not directly behind it.

GROOMING IN A HURRY

If you don't have enough time to groom the horse properly before your lesson, be sure that you at least pick out its hooves and clean the area where the saddle and girth will go. Pebbles in a foot can cause lameness, and dirt under the saddle or girth can cause sores. And if you have to do a hurried grooming before a ride, be sure to do a complete grooming after the ride.

CHAPTER 6

SADDLES AND BRIDLES

Tack is the name riders use for saddles, bridles, and other riding equipment. *Tacking up* means putting the saddle, bridle, and any other equipment on the horse.

If you go to a tack store and look at the new saddles, you will find that they are sold without fittings (the girth, stirrup leathers, and stirrups). These come separately. At a riding stable, however, the saddles will have the fittings already attached, and each saddle may be used on several horses during an average day. Each horse will have its own saddle pad, just the way each horse has its own grooming equipment. The saddle pad goes between the horse and the saddle. It keeps the underside of the saddle clean and provides a little extra cushioning for the horse's back. The saddle pad should always be clean.

THE RIGHT TACK FOR YOU

Different riding disciplines require different saddles. Jumping, dressage, hunting, and eventing all have their own particular requirements.

There are specialized saddles for jumping that have flat seats and forward-cut flaps, which are wonderful for show jumping but not useful for dressage or cross-country riding. There are specialized saddles for dressage that have deeper seats and straight flaps, which are wonderful for dressage but not useful for jumping. And then there are saddles that are designed to be used for more than one sport: basic dressage *and* basic show-jumping *and* cross-country riding. These are the "eventing" or "all-purpose" saddles, the most useful saddles for beginner riders.

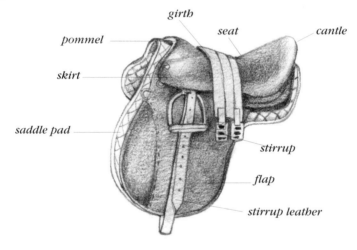

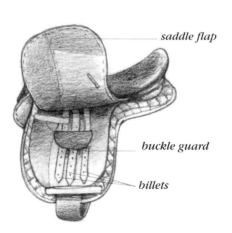

All-purpose saddle

In a year or two, if you decide to focus on one particular riding discipline, you may want to use a saddle that's designed for that particular activity, such as dressage or jumping. But during your first year of lessons, a good all-purpose saddle will suit your needs perfectly. Ask your instructor about the different saddles in the tack room, and look at saddles in catalogs and when you visit tack shops. You will quickly learn to recognize the various kinds of saddles.

TACKING UP

Watch when your instructor tacks up your horse, because you will probably do this yourself after the first few lessons. The first thing that goes on the horse is the saddle pad. Shake it out and look at it before you put it on the horse so that you can be sure it is clean and smooth. A dirty or sweaty pad, or one that is lumpy, can cause a horse to develop a sore back, so inspect your horse's saddle pad carefully. Then, if the pad is clean and dry, place it high on the horse's back, toward the neck and on the shoulders. You'll probably think it's too far forward, and you'll be right. Don't worry, you'll move it back after saddling the horse.

How to Saddle a Horse

Next, look at the saddle. The girth will be buckled to the saddle on the right side, and it will be lying across the saddle. Lift the saddle high up, onto the horse's shoulders, so that the saddle is on top of the saddle pad. Pull the front of the saddle pad up into the saddle gullet. Then hold the saddle with both hands—right hand holding the cantle and the back of the pad, left hand holding the pommel and the front of the pad—and slide the saddle and pad back together until the saddle sits level, with the pommel behind the horse's withers. By putting the pad too far forward and then sliding the saddle and pad back into place,

Don't Pinch Your Horse!

When you have fastened the girth, you can make your horse much more comfortable by lifting each of the horse's front legs in turn and pulling it forward. This pulls the skin just behind the horse's elbows out from under the girth. Pulling this skin makes it smooth and takes out any wrinkles that could be pinched by the girth and hurt the horse. Also, if your saddle is still placed just a little bit too far forward, pulling the front legs out will help shift the saddle back into exactly the right place on the horse's back.

you have smoothed the horse's hair under the saddle to make it more comfortable.

Now, walk around the horse to its right side and check to see that the saddle is straight and the pad is smooth, not bunched up. Lift the girth off the saddle and check to be sure that its underside—the side that will be against the horse—is clean and smooth. If it looks good, let it hang straight down. Walk around the horse again, to its left side, then reach underneath and bring the girth up to the left side of the saddle. Lift the flap of the saddle (you may need to rest it on your head, because you will probably need both hands to fasten the girth), and fasten the two girth buckles to the first and third billet straps. (The middle one is a spare.) Just fasten the girth at first, using the first, lowest holes on the billets to begin with, so that the horse can get used to the pressure before you tighten the girth. You will tighten the girth a little bit in just a few minutes, and you'll need to check it again to see whether it needs tightening just before you mount. Your instructor will probably remind you of this, but you should get into the habit of checking your horse's girth.

How to Bridle a Horse

Bridles can look very complicated when you aren't used to them. Watch your instructor carefully the first few times he or she bridles your horse so that you'll know what to do when it's your turn to put on the bridle.

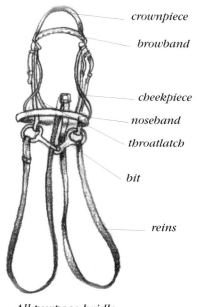

crownpiece

browband

cheekpiece

noseband

throatlatch

bit

reins

All-purpose bridle

First, be sure that the cavesson (noseband) and throatlatch are both unbuckled. You will buckle these later. The cavesson always buckles under the horse's jaw, and the throatlatch buckle should always be on the left side of the horse's head.

Next, standing on the horse's left side, take the reins and put them *over* the horse's neck so that you have something with which to hold the horse. Then unfasten the halter and slip it off the horse's face. Hold the top of the bridle—the crownpiece—in your right hand, and use your left hand to spread the bit so that it is flat. Put your right hand on your horse's forehead so that you can pull the bridle up smoothly over its ears as soon as it takes the bit. If the horse opens its mouth for the bit, slide it in gently without bumping his teeth, and be sure that its tongue is *under* the bit. You can use your left thumb to touch the corner of its mouth if the horse doesn't open it right away. If your thumb is touching his mouth and it still doesn't open wide, put your thumb inside the corner of the mouth and press it against the gum.

When the bit is in the horse's mouth, you can pull the top of the bridle over its ears. Do it gently and quietly—ears are sensitive! Be careful not to rub the leather over the horse's eyes. Once the bridle is in place, adjust it evenly and check to be sure that the browband doesn't rub its ears, and that it doesn't have pieces of its mane tangled in the bridle.

Now you can fasten the cavesson and throatlatch. Fasten them both loosely. The cavesson should be under the cheekpieces, and you must be careful to fasten it underneath the cheekpieces instead of over them. If you fastened the cavesson over the bridle's cheekpieces, it would interfere with the bit. When the cavesson and throatlatch are fastened, there should be room for you to put two fingers comfortably between the cavesson and the horse's nose, and a fist between the throatlatch and the horse's cheek.

Now your horse is tacked up!

UNTACKING YOUR HORSE

After your ride, you will need to untack the horse. It's very much like tacking up, only in reverse. Have your halter ready. Undo the cavesson buckle and the throatlatch buckle, but leave the reins around the horse's neck. Put your right hand up behind the horse's ears so that you can hold the crownpiece and slip it forward over the horse's ears. Place your left hand on top of the horse's nose to remind it to hold still. Don't move too quickly; instead, lower your right hand *slowly*, giving the horse time to open its mouth so that the bit doesn't hit his teeth on the way out of its mouth.

When the bridle is off, put on the horse's halter. Now you can take the reins over the horse's head and tie it up by the halter.

Put the bridle back where you found it, and come back for the saddle. Stand on the horse's left side and lift the saddle flap. Undo both girth buckles, but don't drop the girth—it can bang the horse's legs and frighten or hurt it. Hold it in your left hand and lower it gently.

When it is hanging straight down, walk around to the right side of the horse, pick up the hanging girth, and put it over the top of the saddle. Then walk back to the horse's left side and take the saddle off. If the horse or pony is small, you can lift the saddle off. If the horse or pony is tall, you should still lift it a little before you slide it off. If you just pull the saddle off sideways, it will bang against the horse's spine. The most important thing to remember is to hold the saddle carefully, with your left hand on the pommel and your right hand on the cantle. Then put the saddle back on the saddle rack where you found it.

Before returning your horse to its stall, it should once again be groomed. This time, wipe down any sweaty areas, such as under the saddle and behind the elbows, with a damp cloth. Give your horse a good once-over with a body brush, and pick its hooves again to remove any pebbles that may have accumulated during your ride.

After you have put the horse back in its stall or field, removed its halter, and checked to be sure that it has water to drink, come back to the tack room and wipe the bit clean, then wipe the bridle and saddle leather with a damp cloth to remove sweat and arena dust.

CLEANING TACK

If you are allowed to help clean the tack, you can learn a lot about how it is put together, and you can learn how to check tack for safety.

Tack should be cleaned and conditioned regularly, not just because clean, shiny tack looks nice but because it's safe. Dirty tack can make your horse sore. It can also be dangerous! Dry, brittle tack can break. Over-oiled, too-soft tack can stretch and pull apart, and the stitching can rot from the excess oil.

Clean tack is important to your horse. Your bit should be cleaned (washed, rinsed, and dried) after each ride. Asking a horse to open its mouth for a dirty, crusty bit is like asking you to eat your lunch with a dirty, crusty fork! Saddles and bridles should be wiped clean after each ride, and bridles should be taken apart and cleaned thoroughly once a week. Your instructor will show you how to use a barely damp sponge and special saddle soap to care for the leather. Tack-cleaning time is also a good opportunity to safety-check your tack.

CHECKING TACK FOR SAFETY

When you tack up a horse, it's easy to check the tack for safety. When you fasten your girth, you'll notice if the girth is cracked, if the elastic ends are worn or frayed, and if any stitching is loose or missing. Also look at the billet straps. If they are cracked or broken, they are unsafe. If the holes in the billet straps are pulled long and narrow instead of small and round, mention it to your instructor—it is time to replace those billets. The stirrup leathers should be checked, too.

If they are cracked and dry, or if there is any broken, loose, or missing stitching, they are unsafe. While you're looking at the stirrup leathers, take a good look at the stirrup bars. The safety catches should be down, in the open position—not up, in the closed position. When you bridle your horse, you'll probably notice any cracked or broken leather or loose stitching.

Since most of your tacking up is done from the left side, it is important to remember to check the right side, too! A good safety check involves looking at the stirrup leathers, the girth, and the bridle on both sides of the horse.

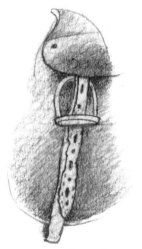

Worn, cracking stirrup leathers are a safety hazard.

Even if you know that the horse you ride always wears the same bridle, check the fit of the bridle when you put it on the horse. Someone may have borrowed it to use on another horse and adjusted the straps differently.

The United States Pony Club (USPC), a popular riding organization, includes safety checks as part of their standard routine. Even if you aren't a member of a Pony Club, it's a good idea to adopt the Pony Club attitude toward safety. Safety checks are important for every rider: beginner, intermediate, and advanced students, as well as instructors. At every mounted meeting and every lesson, each Pony Club rider is given a quick safety check by the instructor. It only takes a few seconds to check that the saddle, bridle, and saddle pad are in place and in good condition, and the girth is snug. It only takes another second to check that the rider's footgear is safe and suitable, and that the safety helmet is in place and fastened. Check your tack and equipment each time you ride—make it a habit. The time to find a problem is *before* you begin your ride.

If you are handed a horse that has already been tacked up by someone else, at your lesson or at a friend's house or on a trailride that you take on vacation, you should take a few minutes to safety-check your tack.

There's another kind of safety that you should check: your horse's comfort! If you find a wrinkled saddle pad, or a saddle flap that's folded up, or a twisted girth, or a bit that's hanging high on one side of the horse's mouth and low on the other, you have found something that is unsafe. If riding makes your horse uncomfortable, he will be inattentive and disobedient, and no matter how hard he tries, he won't be able to do his best. Think of how you would feel at a track meet or tennis match, if you had a rock in one shoe or one shoelace tied too tightly. Discomfort is very distracting! Help your horse pay attention to you by making sure that everything fits well and is adjusted correctly before you mount.

LEADING A TACKED-UP HORSE

When your horse is tacked up and you are leading it to the arena for a lesson, or somewhere else, you should always check for two important safety factors.

1) Be sure that the stirrups aren't dangling. Whenever you dismount, run the stirrups up the leathers. A dangling stirrup can catch on a jump standard, or in a doorway, or on people's clothing as they walk past your horse. A dangling stirrup can also catch on the horse's bit if the horse swings its head around to bite at a fly on his side. And even if none of these things happens, dangling stirrups will thump uncomfortably against the horse's side.

To run a stirrup up its leather, first pull out the leather as though you were checking to see whether it's the right length for you. Instead of holding the stirrup, hold the end of the leather loop nearest your body, and slide the stirrup up the underside of the loop, all the way to the stirrup bar on the saddle. Then take the whole loop and tuck it through the stirrup. This will keep the stirrup in place while you lead the horse.

2) Don't try to lead your horse while the reins are still around its neck. Always take the reins over the horse's head, even if you are leading it for just a short distance. With the whole length of the reins in your hands, you can keep a double grip on the reins. With your right hand holding the reins about six inches from the bit, and your left hand holding the reins near the buckle, you have much more control over

the horse. If the reins are very long, fold their ends and hold them in your left hand, but never wrap the reins around your hand.

CHAPTER 7

RIDING A HORSE

The first step to riding, of course, is getting on your horse! But there are a few safety procedures you should always follow before getting on. Before you mount your horse, be sure that your safety helmet is on properly, with the harness fastened. Keep it fastened until your ride is over and you have dismounted. Never unfasten the harness and let it hang loose while you are still on your horse.

Now check your horse's girth by sliding your hand underneath it. If there is a lot of extra room, you will want to tighten it before you mount so that the saddle doesn't slip sideways while you are getting on. The girth usually needs to be tightened a hole or two before you mount, and it may need to be tightened another hole after you've been riding for about fifteen minutes. If the girth isn't snug when you mount, the saddle will pull down toward you when you put your weight in the stirrup, and you'll be riding the horse's side! So always check your girth before you mount. When you have checked the girth, pull the stirrups down.

MOUNTING

When you are ready, put the reins over your horse's neck and stand by its left shoulder, facing its tail. Shorten the reins so that you have a very light feel of the horse's mouth. Hold both reins and a handful of the horse's mane in your left hand. With your right hand, take the stirrup and turn it toward you so that you can put the ball of your left foot into the stirrup. Now you are standing on your right foot, with your left foot in the stirrup. Take your right hand and hold the pommel of the saddle—now you are facing the horse's left side. Bend your right knee, bounce a time or two if you need to, and then jump *up*, so that you are standing in your left stirrup, holding yourself up over the saddle by taking as much weight as possible on your arms. Swing your right leg high so that it goes over the saddle, then sit down very gently and find your right stirrup with your right foot. When you can do all this very smoothly, you'll be able to find your right stirrup *before* you sit down.

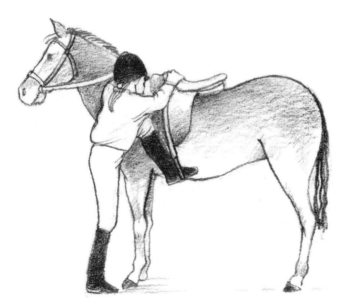

*To mount, begin by placing your left foot in the stirrup
while grasping the pommel.*

61

Mounting Manners Matter

Mounting a horse is like shaking hands with a person—it's an introduction, and it creates a first impression. Mounting gives the horse its first impression of you as a rider. If you mount smoothly and quietly, and settle into the saddle lightly and quietly, your horse's first impression of you will be a good one!

Helpful hints for mounting

If your horse steps sideways away from you as you mount, shorten the right rein to bend its neck slightly to the right. If your horse moves sideways now, it will have to move toward you instead of away from you.

If your horse wants to move forward as you mount, be sure that your left toe is turned toward the *girth*, not toward the horse's side. You can't blame the horse for starting to walk if you poke or kick it in the side with your foot—after all, horses have been taught to go forward when the rider does that.

It may seem silly to begin by facing the horse's rear, but there's a good reason for this position. If the horse takes a step or two forward while you mount, you will still be able to swing yourself up into the saddle. This doesn't work as well if you stand behind the girth facing forward—in fact, it puts you in an unsafe position. If the horse moves forward, you are left behind it, perhaps with one foot caught in the stirrup.

BASIC RIDING POSITION

When you first sit down in the saddle, you may feel insecure and think that you need to hang onto something—the reins, the mane, the saddle. However, you don't need to hang on. You need to learn to stay on by using your balance, just the way you use it when you walk or run or climb stairs.

Sit in the deepest part of your saddle—the middle. Your weight should be in your thighs, not in your bottom. Riding position is not really a sitting position, although we talk about the rider's "seat." Riding position is the position you would be in if you stood on the ground with your legs apart and your knees bent.

When you are in the saddle, your lower legs should be positioned so that your feet are directly under your knees. Your instructor will help you find the correct position. It will feel strange at first, but don't worry—if you practice, it will feel natural very soon.

Basic riding position

Lopsided? Check Your Stirrups!

It's very important to keep your stirrup leathers adjusted to the same length. If one is longer than the other, you won't be able to achieve a correct, straight position. Your weight will be unbalanced and you will sit lopsided and feel insecure. Keep your stirrup leathers even, and don't rely on the numbers stamped into the leather even if the leathers are fairly new. If you clean tack at the barn, make a habit of switching the stirrup leathers every week, putting the left leather on the right side and the right leather on the left side. Since the left-side

When your instructor places your feet in the stirrups, you will notice that the stirrup goes right across the ball of your foot and that your heel is lower than your toe. This is important, because with your heel low, your legs can stay steady and your ankles can act as shock absorbers. If you stand on your toes and let your heels come up, you lose that flexibility in the ankle and its shock-absorbing effect.

Your stirrups need to be at the right height for you. Before you mount, you can measure them against your arm to get an approximate idea of the right length. Close one hand and put your arm straight out with your knuckles against the stirrup bar. With your other hand, hold the stirrup and pull it out so that the leather is straight along your arm. The bottom of the stirrup should touch your armpit. When you are mounted, take both feet out of the stirrups for a moment and let your legs hang naturally. Where does the bottom of the stirrup touch your leg? It should touch your anklebone. If your stirrups are a little too long or too short, you can adjust them from the saddle.

Your back should be straight, not arched. Your head should be up, with your eyes looking ahead of you, between the horse's ears.

Your upper arms should hang down easily and naturally from your shoulders, with no tension. Your elbows should be bent, so that your lower arms and hands are out in front of your body, with your hands about four inches above the withers and about four inches apart.

Your hands should be closed on the reins. Your instructor will show you how to hold your reins and how to shorten and lengthen them. Keep your hands in "soft" fists, so that you can just feel your fingers touching your palms. If you squeeze your hands, making "hard" fists, your arms will feel stiff and tense, and you won't be able to follow your horse's head and neck movements. If you let your fingers open, your rein contact will be unpredictable and your horse will be uncomfortable, never knowing what to expect from you.

Your thumbs should be up but not straight up—they should point toward the base of your horse's opposite ears. If you drop your eyes for a moment to look at your thumbs, you should see your left thumb pointing at the base of your horse's right ear, and your right thumb

leather stretches more than the right-side leather (because we mount from the left), letting each leather be on the left side half of the time will help keep both leathers the same length.

Keeping the Reins Even

If your horse seems to keep wanting to turn in one direction or the other, check your reins. They may be uneven, and without being aware of it, you may be asking the horse to turn one way all the time! Sometimes it's useful to tie little pieces of colorful yarn on each rein to mark the places where you will hold them at a walk and a trot.

pointing at the base of your horse's left ear. There is a reason for this: If you hold your arms, hands, and reins correctly, you will find it easy to let your arms follow the movements of the horse's head. At a walk and at a canter, the horse moves its head and neck to balance itself; by following the horse's movements, you give it the freedom to stay balanced and comfortable. At a trot, the horse carries its head a little higher and a little nearer its body, and it does *not* use its head and neck for balance. Your instructor will remind you to shorten your reins before you ask your horse to trot.

Remember that you want to be a horseman, not just a rider. A horseman always thinks of the horse first and is never brutal or unkind to a horse. Sometimes you may feel very frustrated, but whatever you do, don't yank or jerk the reins. A true horseman will *never, ever* punish a horse with the bit.

When you want to reward your horse, a gentle pat, a soft word, and a little scratch on the withers will all be appreciated.

RIDING AT A WALK, TROT, AND CANTER

Walking

Riding at a walk is easy and fun. All you need to do is sit up straight and let the horse move you along. A quiet, calm, steady walk is the perfect gait to let you get used to sitting on a horse. The walk has an easy rhythm to follow, and if you relax your back, you can feel how the horse moves and how your back moves with it.

The walk is also the best gait for you to learn two very important parts of riding: how to use your eyes and how to follow your horse's mouth with your hands. Your eyes are important—they should look up, out, and ahead so that you know where you are going next. And your hands are important, too. The reins are like telephone lines, there to help you communicate with your horse. They aren't handles or safety straps, so don't pull them or hang on them. At the walk, your horse's head will move forward and down, then back and up, over and over again. The reins will move with its head, and your arms should move with the reins. You'll feel your elbows opening and closing—that's good!

Position Poem

There's an old English verse that young riders learned to help them remember correct position:

Your head and your heart–keep up!

Your hands and your heels–keep down!

Your legs press into your horse's sides,

Your elbows into your own.

Trotting

When you feel completely comfortable, relaxed, and at ease while your horse is walking, you are ready to try trotting. Trotting is faster and bumpier than walking. At first, you will feel as though you are just bouncing hard against the saddle. Your instructor will teach you to "post" or "rise" to the trot, which means sitting every other beat instead of every beat. Posting makes trotting much more comfortable. You can count the beats by saying "one-two" or "up-down." At the trot, the horse doesn't move its head, so you can keep your hands and reins very steady. You can even grab a handful of mane to steady yourself—the horse won't mind at all. Trotting isn't hard if you let the horse do most of the work. The horse's movement will bounce you up—all you have to do is move a little forward at the same time, then come back to the saddle gently and let the horse bounce you up again. Your back should be straight, and you will lean slightly forward as you come up. Your eyes should be looking up, out, and ahead, and your lower legs should be steady and quiet, like your hands.

Posting Diagonals

When you can post easily, your instructor will talk to you about diagonals. When the horse is trotting, it is moving from one diagonal pair of legs (the front leg on one side and the hind leg on the other side) to the other, back and forth. That's why each trot stride has two beats. Your instructor will want you to post on the outside diagonal, which means that the "up" part of your "up-down" should be timed with the horse's outside foreleg. *Outside* means on the side of the arena wall; *inside* means on the side toward the center of the arena. When the horse's outside foreleg comes forward, you should be coming *up*. The easiest way to remember this rule is to tell yourself, "Rise and fall with the leg on the wall."

The rider is posting on the left diagonal; that is, she is rising with the horse's left foreleg.

Changing Diagonals

When you change directions, and your other side is toward the wall, you will want to change your posting diagonal, too, so that you will still be able to "rise and fall with the leg on the wall." There are two different ways of changing your diagonal easily and smoothly. Try them both—you may find that one method is easier for you than the other.

Method #1: Sitting an extra beat. While you are posting and telling yourself "up-down, up-down," you can change diagonals by staying in the saddle for one more beat. As you post, tell yourself "up-down, up-down, up-down-*down*, up-down." Sitting for one extra "down" beat will start you posting on the other diagonal.

Staying Relaxed

Whenever you get nervous or insecure, sit up straight, look straight ahead, take a deep breath, and let it out slowly through your mouth, smile, and feel your whole body relax.

Method #2: Staying out of the saddle for an extra beat. This method is definitely less bumpy than sitting the extra beat, but it may not be as easy for you to know when to start posting again. Using this method, you post and tell yourself "up-down, up-down," and then change your diagonal by staying *up* for one more beat: "up-down, up-down, up-*up*-down, up-down." Holding an extra "up" beat will start you posting on the other diagonal.

If you are doing your best and keep coming back to the same diagonal again and again, exaggerate your posting a little so that you are moving a little higher and a little more forward. While you do that, say your "up-down, up-down" posting rhythm out loud. That will help you sit— or stay up—for only *one* more beat, so that you can change your posting diagonal easily. Sitting two beats ("down-down") or staying up for two beats ("up-up") will put you on the new diagonal, but if you accidentally sit or stay up for *three* beats ("down-down-down" or "up-up-up"), you will always end up right back on the same diagonal you started from.

Cantering

Your instructor will tell you when he or she thinks you are ready to canter. You'll have a pleasant surprise: Cantering is much easier than trotting! It's a little faster, but it has a comfortable rhythm ("one-two-three-pause, one-two-three-pause") and you'll find it easy to sit to that rhythm. Cantering is a little like walking, because you stay in your saddle and let your arms move with your horse's head. And like the walk, the canter calls for a rider to sit tall with a relaxed lower back.

If cantering frightens you, ask your instructor to teach you on the longe line so that you won't have to worry about steering your horse while you learn to sit the canter. If you are in a group of riders, ask to canter alone while the others stand in the middle of the ring. It's much less frightening when it doesn't feel like a horse race.

EXERCISES FOR RIDERS

Your instructor will know a lot of exercises to help you with specific fears, stiffness, or riding problems. There are some easy exercises that all riders can do to improve their position and balance.

Bending Exercise

While someone holds your horse, get into a good riding position, then keep your legs in place and lean your upper body forward until your chest touches your horse's mane. Then straighten up—keeping those legs in place!—and slowly lean backward until your helmet touches your horse's back. Then straighten up again. When you can do this without moving your legs, you'll be on your way to a steady leg and a supple, independent upper body.

Back-Stretching Exercise

While someone holds your horse, bend forward from the hips, reach forward with both arms, and stretch until you touch your horse's ears, then slowly sit up again and let your arms come back to you slowly. Keep your legs in position underneath you while you do this.

Shoulder-Loosening Exercise

At a halt, stretch out your arms one at a time, from the shoulder, and circle them slowly while keeping your legs quiet and in the correct position.

Hip-Stretching Exercise

While someone holds your horse, put both arms straight out at your sides, at shoulder level. Keep your legs steady while you turn your whole torso, arms, and head slowly from side to side. Keep your arms straight and high, and twist so that one hand is pointing toward your

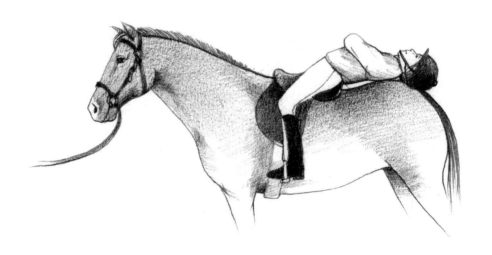

Bending exercise

horse's ears and the other one toward its tail. You'll feel a stretch through your whole body as you turn.

FALLING OFF

Many beginner riders are terrified of the idea of falling off; others can't wait to fall off, because they've heard that they can't be a real rider until they've fallen off several times. *You* can be more sensible! Every rider, even professional show riders and jockeys who ride for a living, is going to fall off sometime. It's part of riding, but smart riders won't fall off any more often than they have to.

You can learn to fall, just as you can learn any other skill. If you've ever had a gymnastics or tumbling class, you already know how to tuck and roll. If you haven't, you might consider taking a few "falling" lessons. It's fun and can make you feel much more secure.

Your helmet is there to protect your head, but you have other body parts to protect—your fingers and hands, for instance! If you bring your arms close to your chest and curl over them as you fall, you won't risk breaking a finger or wrist by landing on it. Whatever you do, don't put out an arm to try to break the fall!

Emergency Dismounts

You will learn how to jump off and away from your horse at a halt, then at a walk, a trot, and perhaps even a canter. Knowing how to do this can make you feel much more secure about accidental falls. One easy way to practice emergency dismounts is "by the numbers": On "one," you kick your feet free of the stirrups and put your hands on the horse's neck; on "two," you lean forward, sliding your arms around the horse's neck and straightening your legs behind you; and on "three" you slide down the horse's left side, letting go of its neck as your feet touch the ground. There are several different ways of performing emergency dismounts. Your instructor may have a different way of teaching this—just ask!

You'll break something, all right, but it will probably be your collarbone.

Let your horse go if you fall. Don't try to hold onto the reins—it's better if your horse keeps moving so that its hooves will be nowhere near you. Horses will try to avoid stepping on fallen riders, so make it easy for them by rolling up in a ball, with no arms or legs sticking out!

GETTING BACK ON

There's an old saying that riders who fall off a horse should get right back on. This isn't always true, and it isn't always safe. If you fall off and are sure that you are okay, your instructor will probably let you get back on the horse. If you aren't sure that you're okay, or if the instructor is worried that you might not be okay, he or she will probably want you to stay where you are until help comes. Try to cooperate, even if you think that you're just fine and the instructor is being silly. The riding stable and the instructor may be legally required to keep a fallen rider quiet and call emergency services. And if the rider is hurt, everyone will be very glad that the stable had a good procedure to follow in case of accidents.

LEARNING THE AIDS

The natural aids are the legs, seat, hands, and voice. The artificial aids are the whip, spur, and other equipment. During your first year of lessons, you should use only the natural aids. It takes time to learn to use your aids correctly. There is a correct aid, or combination of aids, for everything you could ever want your horse to do. Your job as a rider is to learn those aids and practice using them correctly, gently, and softly.

Legs

When you use your legs to signal your horse, give a brief, soft squeeze with your lower legs. Try to keep your heels down, and squeeze with your calves. A brief squeeze with *both* legs tells the horse that you want it to move forward; a squeeze with *one* leg tells the horse that you want it to move sideways, away from that leg.

If your horse doesn't respond to your leg squeeze, don't kick it and don't keep squeezing. Relax, wait a moment, and repeat the squeeze. The horse will get the idea. Some horses respond to almost no squeeze at all; some need a strong squeeze. Always start with a gentle aid!

Carrying a Crop

Some school horses can be very slow and sleepy with beginner riders on board, and it's possible that your instructor may give you a small whip, called a riding crop, when you ride certain horses. Some crops have a loop of leather or plastic at one end. This is called a wrist loop, but you should never put it over your wrist. It's a dangerous thing to do. If the crop catches on something while the loop is around your wrist, you can end up with a sprained or broken wrist! So, if the riding crop belongs to you, cut the loop off. If the crop belongs to the instructor or the riding stable, ask if you can use plastic tape or electrician's tape to stick the loop to the handle so that you won't forget and put your wrist through it. You can still have a loop, though. If you're worried about dropping your riding crop, make a loop from a long, thin rubber band or a piece of thin string. If the riding crop catches on anything, this kind of loop will break before you can get hurt.

Seat

Your seat, or weight, is a useful aid. Leaning forward, like a jockey on a race-horse, will tell your horse that you want it to move forward or go faster. Sitting up straight will slow the horse down and make it easier for it to stop. The faster you go, the more you will lean forward, just as you do when you are on foot. On foot, you stand straight when you aren't moving, lean a little forward when you walk, lean a little more forward when you jog, and even more forward when you run. On horseback, your body position, balance, and seat/weight aids should match what your horse is doing or what you want it to do.

Hands

You already know how to follow the horse's head movements with your hands and arms. Now, if you want to signal the horse with the reins, you can use your hands actively. Remember that your horse is paying attention to *all* of your aids, and that you need to be very clear about what you want. Increasing the pressure on both reins tells the horse that you want it to stop. Increasing the pressure on both reins, leaning slightly forward, and squeezing with both legs tells the horse that you want it to trot. Squeeze your hands briefly to increase the rein pressure—never pull! Always remember that there is a sensitive mouth at the other end of the reins.

Voice

Your voice is a powerful aid. Horses appreciate praise, especially when it is offered in a gentle voice. School horses generally know and respond to the command "Whoa!" You can use that word loudly and commandingly to mean "Stop!" or you can say it more softly and slowly to mean "Slow down, please." Most school horses also know many other commands such as "Walk," "Trot," and "Canter," so you can use the words to reinforce your other aids. But don't use them too loudly, because you don't want to cause someone else's horse to change gaits unexpectedly!

*Leaning slightly forward and tightening the legs are a
signal to your horse to increase its speed.*

I Need to Tighten My Girth!

If, as you ride along, you realize that you need to tighten your girth or adjust your stirrups, go to the center of the arena and stop. Then make your adjustments. Your horse will be able to stand out of the way of the other horses, and you'll be able to make your adjustments without worrying about other horses bumping into you.

RIDING ARENA ETIQUETTE

When you are riding in a group lesson, or just sharing an arena with other riders, you need to observe some simple rules of etiquette. If you're new to riding and if the rules aren't posted in the arena or your instructor doesn't remember to tell you, here are some typical arena rules and some useful suggestions.

If you are the only rider in your lesson, you can enter the arena and begin riding in whatever direction and at whatever gait suits you and your instructor. If you and several other riders are sharing a lesson, you will probably lead your horses into the arena at the same time and mount up at the same time. If you are joining a group lesson in progress, or if you are entering the arena to ride when other people are already riding there, you will need to let the others know that you are about to join them. Look around, and time your entrance for a moment when the area near the door is clear. Before you lead or ride your horse into the arena, call out "Door," "Gate," "Coming in," or whatever makes sense (your stable may have a particular term to use). What's important is that no one is surprised and that there are no collisions. When you enter the arena, mount quietly and begin riding in the same direction as the other riders. If you're in a lesson, the instructor will ask all of you to change direction periodically. If you're just riding with others in the same arena and you would like to go in the other direction, just ask. If you ask, "Could we reverse, please?" the other riders will usually be glad to agree.

Paying attention is always an important safety factor when horses are involved, and this is certainly true when you are sharing an arena. Be aware of what is going on around you, and of where the other horses and riders are and where they are going. Keep your distance from the next rider, and keep the horse you are riding away from the other horses. Horses that crowd other horses can get kicked or bitten, so don't let your horse put its nose near another horse's nose or crowd up against another horse's tail.

If you are in a lesson, of course you will be paying close attention to your instructor, but you'll need to keep your own eyes open, too. If you are riding on the rail, keep a safe distance—at least two horse-lengths—from the rider in front of you. The rider in back of you will keep two lengths back, and so on. If everyone is trotting or cantering and your horse is much faster than the others, try to keep it trotting or cantering more slowly. If you can't keep your horse at a safe distance from the horse in front of you, make a circle and come back to the rail at a safe distance behind the last rider. When the instructor asks for a change of direction, be sure that you know *how* he or she wants you to change direction, and try to do it at the same time as the other riders. If everyone changes direction at once, you'll all find yourselves on the rail going the other way, very smoothly. But if some riders turn away from the rail and make a large circle to change direction while other riders turn toward the rail and make a small circle and still other riders go across the arena, things can get very disorganized.

Find out exactly what your instructor wants you to do when he or she says "Change direction," and ask the instructor to give all the students a chance to practice doing it smoothly and promptly. If some people change direction immediately and some don't, there will be two lines of riders meeting each other nose-to-nose!

If you are coming up behind a slower rider and need to pass, give your horse plenty of room and let the other rider know what you are about to do. Call out "Rail" if you are passing on the outside, and

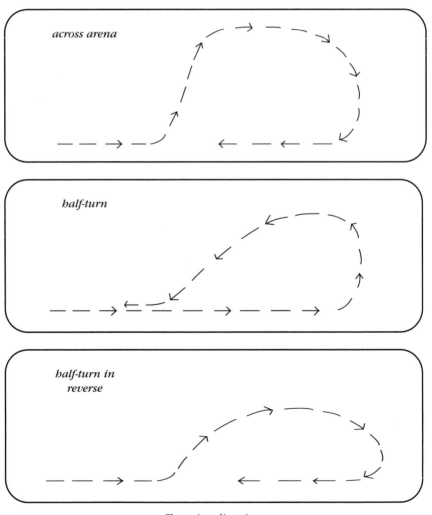

Changing directions

"Inside" if you are passing on the inside. And give the other horse and rider more room than you think they need—pass wide, as if you were driving a very large truck.

Use your voice with care. If you need to say something to the other riders, speak up. If you need to say something to your own horse, speak very softly. You already know that saying "Trot" loudly may help you get your horse into a trot but might get someone else's horse into a trot, too! Making kissing, and clucking, and clicking sounds to encourage your horse can also cause other horses to respond to the sounds, so try to use your other aids (legs and seat) instead.

Keep an eye out for the other horses and riders, and use your ears, too. You may not be able to see what is going on behind you, but you can listen for sounds of something happening where you can't see it. If one rider is out of control or falls off, all the other riders should stop their horses and wait quietly until the instructor starts the class again. If someone's horse is running away, the rider should shout "Heads up!" so that everyone else in the arena can pay attention. If a rider falls off and the horse trots away, the rider or

Two-Lane Traffic

If you need to ride your horse tracking left when everyone else is tracking right, or if you are doing figures while other riders are on the rail or vice versa, remember that riders facing each other should always pass left shoulder to left shoulder. Remembering "left-to-left" will save you some bumpy surprises!

someone else should call out "Loose horse!" so that the other riders in the arena will know to stop and stand.

"COOLING OUT" YOUR HORSE

After your lesson, if you did a lot of cantering or jumping, your horse may be hot and sweating. If so, your instructor will ask you to "cool him out." This means walking the horse around until it is no longer too hot, breathing hard, or sweating. When the horse is cooled out, it will be relaxed, and then you will be able to give it a good post-ride grooming.

In the summer, you may be able to give your horse a rinse with plain water, or a bath. In the winter, you can't give the horse a bath, but you can rub the sweaty areas with a hot, damp towel and then cover the horse with a blanket and walk it until its coat is dry.

DISMOUNTING

When you are ready to dismount, take your right foot out of the stirrup, put your reins in your left hand, and lean that hand on the horse's neck. Now lean your right hand against the pommel. Stand on your left stirrup and swing your right leg over the horse so that you are supporting your weight on your two hands. Lean your body against the saddle so that you are lying across it with your head and upper body on the right and your legs on the left. While you are still lying over the saddle, take your left foot *out* of the stirrup. Finally, straighten your upper body and let yourself slide down the horse's side with your knees slightly bent, landing on both feet. This gets easier with practice!

When you dismount at the end of your lesson, you will want to do three more things: Run the stirrups up the leathers, loosen the girth and take the reins over the horse's head so that you can use them to lead him.

CHAPTER 8

JUMPING

When you have learned to walk, trot, and canter and are comfortable riding several different horses at the riding school, you will probably want to learn to jump. Most riders enjoy jumping very much and look forward to the day when their instructor thinks that they are ready for their first jumping lesson.

Although it's important to be able to canter comfortably before you begin jumping, there are a lot of exercises you can do on horseback to prepare you for jumping, even before you learn to canter.

IMPROVING YOUR LEG

As soon as you are comfortable steering and posting at the trot, you can begin to make your legs steadier. Steady legs are a very important requirement for riders who want to jump!

One of the best exercises for your legs is to spend as much time as you can in your two-point position. The two-point position or "half-seat" is the position you are in when you do the "up" part of your posting trot. When you are in a two-point position, your seat is out of your saddle, but just barely, with your legs resting against the horse's sides and your weight going through your legs into your dropped heels. When you are in a half-seat, you are *not* standing in your stirrups! Remember that you should never stand in your stirrups or push hard against your stirrups or straighten your knees—your ankles and knees need to stay very flexible so that they can absorb the movement when the horse is walking, trotting, cantering, and jumping.

JUMPING POSITION

You can begin practicing getting into your jumping position—and holding the position—when your horse is standing still. Fold forward slightly from your hips, and at the same time, let your bottom slip back toward the cantle. This will let you stay balanced, very close to your saddle, with your knees bent and your weight in your heels. When you go over each jump, you should get *closer* to your saddle, not farther

Two-point position

away from it! Instead of stiffening your joints and standing up, allow your joints to relax, let your heels sink down a little more, and let your seat sink back toward the saddle. The horse, not the rider, should do the jumping.

If it's easy to get up out of the saddle but when you bend forward you feel as though you are about to fall on your horse's neck, you may be looking down—or your legs may be out behind you. Keep your head and eyes up, look out instead of down, check your leg position, and try again.

If you feel too tall and too insecure when you come up out of your saddle, you may be straightening your knees and standing on your stirrups. Try to "float" just barely above your saddle, with your knees bent and relaxed, and your weight in your heels. A good jumping position doesn't mean standing up; it means folding down.

If you feel as if you are rocking forward and backward, you may be pinching with your knees. When you do this, you usually have no weight in your heels. Relax your knees and feel your heels drop and your position become more secure.

Jumping Position Troubleshooting

If it's hard for you to get out of your saddle, you may be trying to fold from the waist instead of the hips, or your legs may be out in front of you. Check your leg position and try again.

Now repeat the two-point position exercise at the walk. At the walk, you can practice balancing over your legs, keeping your seat close to the saddle and letting your weight drop into your heels. Be sure to take a handful of your horse's mane so that you won't pull on the reins if your horse stumbles or if your legs get tired and you have to sit down suddenly. And try to ease yourself back into the saddle before you get too tired—your horse won't appreciate it if you thump down on its back suddenly, especially if you pull on the reins at the same time.

A neck strap can be very helpful to you and the horse while you are learning to ride in a two-point position. Ask your instructor if he or she will put a neck strap on your horse. An old stirrup leather will do very nicely. If you can hold the strap, you won't be in any danger of pulling on your horse's mouth, and your horse will be able to relax and move forward comfortably and with confidence. It takes a little time for most riders to learn how to ride comfortably in a two-point position, staying relaxed and allowing their "shock absorbers"—ankles, knees, and hips—to absorb the movement and the bounce. While you are learning, it's best to use a neck strap, but if you don't have one, you can lean your hands on the horse's neck while you practice your two-point position.

JUMPING RELEASE

Whether you use a neck strap or not, your instructor will want you to learn to perform a "release" as you go between the standards and over the poles. This is when you release your horse's head and neck to move forward as it jumps so that your horse won't get its mouth pulled when it makes the effort to jump. Horses that are allowed to jump in comfort are usually cheerful, eager jumpers; horses that get grabbed in the mouth over or after a jump tend to become unhappy jumpers.

To perform the easiest, most basic release, fasten the neck strap about twelve inches up your horse's neck, or tie a piece of colored yarn in its mane at that level to mark the spot. This is where you will put your hands to let your horse extend its head and neck over the jump. Keep your reins in your hands, push your hands up the horse's neck until you reach the neck strap or the yarn marker, and then use the thumb and first finger on each hand to hold the strap or two pinches of mane. Hold tightly, and keep on holding until after the jump, then let go of the strap or mane and let your hands slide back toward you, gently and slowly. Practice this at a halt, then at the walk, then at the trot, and finally at the canter and over jumps. When this release becomes easy for you, and you no longer need the neck strap to hold or the yarn to remind you to reach forward, you can begin to perform the crest release.

CREST RELEASE

To perform a crest release, you will reach up with your hands just as you did for the basic release, placing them about twelve inches up the horse's neck. With your fingers closed on your reins, you will press your hands against the horse's neck. As long as your hands are pressing hard against your horse's neck, it can stretch its head and neck forward comfortably and make the jumping effort with confidence in its rider. Be careful to press hard—and don't stop pressing until the horse has landed from the jump! If you stop pressing too soon, your hands will jerk back as the horse lands and the bit will hit it in the mouth.

As you become more proficient at jumping, your instructor will teach you other releases: the short release (where your hands stay close to the saddle) and the automatic release (where your hands follow the horse's mouth as it jumps).

EARLY JUMPING LESSONS

When it becomes easy for you to maintain a two-point position at the walk, even during changes of direction, and you no longer need to hold the mane to keep yourself out of the saddle, you can practice the two-point position at the trot. When you can do it easily at the trot, and steer your horse at the same time, you will be ready to canter in a two-point position. And when you are comfortable cantering and steering your horse in a two-point position, you will be ready to learn to jump. Your jumping position is the same as your two-point position or half-seat.

Your first jumping lessons will probably not have real jumps in them. Most instructors will begin by setting up some jump standards with a pole—or even nothing at all—on the ground between them. They will ask you to steer your horse between the standards, just as if you were going to ask your horse to go over an actual jump. This sounds easy, but it can be quite difficult, especially if your instructor sets up a course of several "jumps" and asks you to ride your horse in a particular pattern. Your instructor will ask you to steer straight toward the middle of the jump. When you are very good at doing that, he or she may ask you to go over the right side of one jump, the middle of another, the left side of a third jump, and so on. Doing this at a trot, in your two-point position, takes good balance and concentration. It also takes good use of your eyes! There is a saying, "Look where you're going, because your horse will go where you're looking." Remember this when you are learning to jump, and always look ahead toward where you want to go. When you are trotting toward a jump or pole on the ground, look at it, then look *over* it and plan where you want to go next.

Trotting over ground poles is a good way to prepare for jumping.

JUMPING POSITION CHECKLIST

Remember, when you jump, your position shouldn't change until the horse's movement changes it. You'll jump easily and well if you:

☐ Stay quietly in balance, with your seat just above the saddle.

☐ Keep your eyes up, looking ahead and *over* the jump.

☐ Let all of your shock absorbers do their jobs; allow your weight to sink deep into your heels, and allow your seat to sink back toward your saddle.

☐ Use your release—lean your hands on your horse's neck or hold your neck strap until the horse lands and trots or canters away from the jump.

When you can approach your pretend jumps on a straight line and stop the horse on a straight line, and when you can go over several of these "jumps" while looking up and ahead to see where you are going, your instructor will add a single ground rail between each pair of jump standards. When you are at ease going over these single ground rails, your instructor will replace each ground rail with a small jump. Your horse will know what to do, and *your* job will be to do exactly what you were doing when the jump was a pretend one instead of a real one. Steer your horse straight, keep it moving forward, keep your eyes up, and stay in your two-point position. Don't worry if you spend a lot of time working over poles on the ground. This is how all riders should begin jumping!

Your instructor may change your stirrup length, shortening your stirrups for jumping lessons so that when your legs are hanging down with your feet *out* of the stirrups, the bottom of the stirrup tread will touch just over your anklebones instead of just *at* your anklebones. It may take you some time to adjust to the difference in stirrup length, so don't be surprised if you feel wobbly at first. You'll get used to it, and the new jumping length will begin to feel comfortable and secure.

When your instructor sends you toward your first real jump, it will be a very exciting moment for you. Enjoy it!

CHAPTER 9

HORSE SHOWS

Showing is another activity that can be a lot of fun. Many stables have their own shows, so you can have all the enjoyment of participating without having to get up very early to haul the horses somewhere else. But wherever the show may be, you can go and have a wonderful time if you're prepared.

Getting ready for a show means practicing everything you could possibly be asked to do in the showring. Depending on what sort of show you go to, you could be asked to walk, trot, canter, halt, back up, or perhaps even go over a few small jumps. If you go to a jumper or hunter show, you will have flat classes and, if you jump, over-fences classes. If you go to a dressage show, you will be expected to perform a dressage test alone in an arena. If you go to a small event, you will compete in three different phases: dressage, cross-country, and show jumping. If you go to a gymkhana, or "fun show," you could be asked to do just about anything: jump a row of balloons, participate in a walking race, even push someone else in a wheelbarrow while leading your horse!

Your instructor can tell you exactly what you will need to do at a particular show. He or she can also tell you exactly what you will need to wear. At a fun show or gymkhana, dress will be casual. At a more formal hunter show or dressage show away from your home barn, there is a dress code with which you will want to comply. If your home barn sponsors a show, you will want to dress neatly and appropriately—again, your instructor will be able to help you. And he or she may be able to help with more than just advice—sometimes older students are willing to lend their outgrown show clothes to younger students.

Riding in a show is a very special experience. Riding is the only form of competition in which you and your horse compete as a unit. Showing is teamwork: Everything that happens involves you *and* your horse.

At your first few shows, you shouldn't be worried about strategy. Instead, go early enough to watch some other riders who are doing what you will be doing. Then, when it's

Traditional show clothing includes tall boots, breeches, leather gloves, a collared shirt, and a riding jacket.

your turn to ride, go in and give your horse the very best ride you can, and know that your horse is trying hard, too. When you leave the ring, thank your horse and give it a pat. If you both did your best, that's all that matters.

Remember, you do this for fun! If you get a ribbon, that's great. If you don't, enjoy the day, enjoy your horse, and show sportsmanship. The biggest prize at most schooling shows is a little trophy that's worth about $5. If you don't win this, it isn't the end of the world. And if you take good care of your horse, show it to the best of your ability, and go home pleased with your riding and your horse's efforts, you are a real winner whether you get a ribbon or not.

Don't forget, shows are fun to watch, too! You can have a wonderful day at a horse show just by going to watch. Riding is a great spectator sport, and your family can enjoy it with you when you all attend a big show together.

Chapter 10

RESOURCES FOR YOUNG RIDERS

ASSOCIATIONS

American Horse Shows Association (AHSA)
220 East 42nd Street
New York, NY 10017-5876
(212) 972-2472

American Riding Instructor Certification Program (ARICP)
P.O. Box 282
Alton Bay, NH 03810
(603) 875-4000

American Vaulting Association (AVA)
642 Alford Place
Bainbridge Island, WA 98110-4608
(206) 780-9353
The AVA is the governing body for vaulting
(gymnastics on horseback) in the United States.

American Youth Horse Council, Inc.
4093 Iron Works Pike
Lexington, KY 40511-2742
(800) 879-2942

Association for Horsemanship Safety and Education (CHA)
5318 Old Bullard Road
Tyler, TX 75703
(800) 339-0138

Canadian Equestrian Federation (CEF)
1600 James Naismith Drive
Gloucester, Ontario
K1B 5N4
(613) 748-5632

Canadian Pony Club (CPC)
Box 4256 Station E
Ottawa, Ontario
K1S 5B3
(888) 286-7669

Horsemanship Safety Association, Inc. (HSA)
517 Bear Road
Lake Placid, FL 33852-9726
(941) 465-0289

National 4-H Council
7100 Connecticut Avenue
Chevy Chase, MD 20815-4999
(301) 961-2959
4-H preserves American interest in farming and livestock.

The 4-H Council offers educational programs and activities through many local clubs around the United States.

North American Riding for the Handicapped Association (NARHA)
P.O. Box 33150
Denver, CO 80233
(800) 369-7433
Handicapped people can ride! There are programs all over the United States providing riding opportunities to mentally and physically handicapped persons of all ages.

United States Combined Training Association (USCTA)
P.O. Box 2247
Leesburg, VA 22075
(703) 779-0440

United States Dressage Federation (USDF)
P.O. Box 6669
Lincoln, NE 68506
(402) 434-8550

United States Pony Clubs, Inc. (USPC)
4071 Iron Works Pike
Lexington, KY 40511-8462
(606) 254-7669
Pony Club is international! The United States Pony Club consists of more than 600 clubs throughout the United States, each offering an education in riding and horsemanship for young riders through age twenty-one.

MAGAZINES FOR YOUNG RIDERS

Stable Kids
P.O. Box 1802
Grand Island, NE 68802-1802

Young Equestrian
4905 Mexico Road
St. Peters, MO 63376

Young Rider
P.O. Box 725
Williamsburg, VA 23187-0725

HORSES IN BOOKS (FICTION FOR YOUNG RIDERS)

A Horse by Any Other Name by Jenny Hughes

A Morgan for Melinda by Doris Gates

A New Horse for Marny by Libby Anderson

Annie Learns to Ride by Jennifer Bell

Annie Owns a Pony by Jennifer Bell

Beware the Mare by Jessie Haas

Billy and Blaze (and the rest of the series) by C. W. Anderson

Black Beauty by Anna Sewell

Black Gold by Marguerite Henry

Born to Trot by Marguerite Henry

Fly-by-Night by K. M. Peyton

Justin Morgan Had a Horse by Marguerite Henry

Keeping Barney by Jessie Haas

King of the Wind by Marguerite Henry

Misty of Chincoteague by Marguerite Henry

My Friend Flicka by Mary O'Hara

National Velvet by Enid Bagnold

Plugly: The Horse that Could Do Everything by Cooky McClung

San Domingo: The Medicine Hat Stallion by Marguerite Henry

Stormy, Misty's Foal by Marguerite Henry

The Black Stallion (and the rest of the series, and the
   Flame series) by Walter Farley

The Dark Horse by Jenny Hughes

The Silver Brumby (and the rest of the series) by Elyne Mitchell

HORSES IN BOOKS (NONFICTION FOR YOUNG RIDERS)

Happy Horsemanship by Dorothy Pinch

Safe Horse, Safe Rider by Jessie Haas

The USPC Manual of Horsemanship by Susan E. Harris

Threshold Picture Guides. These are inexpensive illustrated
paperbacks from Kenilworth Press. Some of the most useful
guides for beginner riders are:

Safety

Grooming

Fitting Tack

The Rider's Aids

Flatwork Exercises

Preparing for a Show

Usborne Guides:

Horses and Ponies

Starting Riding

HORSES IN THE MOVIES

Black Beauty

The Black Stallion

The Black Stallion Returns

Born to Run

Casey's Shadow

Champions

Christobalito, the Calypso Colt

Danny

Dark Horse

Gallant Bess

Gypsy Colt

The Horse in the Gray Flannel Suit

The Horse that Played Centerfield

The Horsemasters

International Velvet

Into the West

Ladyhawke

Lightning, the White Stallion

The Littlest Outlaw

The Man from Snowy River

Miracle of the White Stallions

My Friend Flicka

National Velvet

Phar Lap

Return to Snowy River

Ride a Wild Pony

The Rounders

Run Wild, Run Free

The Silver Stallion

Smoky

Sylvester

Thunderhead

Tonka

White Mane

Wild Horse Hank

Wild Hearts Can't Be Broken

The Wild Pony

ON-LINE HORSE RESOURCES

For those of you with Internet access, here are some of
the best horse sites on the World Wide Web:

Jessica Jahiel, Ph.D.: Holistic Horsemanship®
http://www.prairienet.org/jjahiel/

Jessica Jahiel's Horse-sense Electronic Newsletter and Archives
http://www.prairienet.org/horse-sense/

Kris Carroll's Horse Country and Junior Riders Journal
http://www.horse-country.com/

The Haynet (a guide to horse sites on the Internet)
http://www.haynet.net/

American Riding Instructors Association: Directory of Instructors
http://www.win.net/aria/

United States Pony Clubs, Inc.
http://www.ponyclub.org/

CALENDAR OF NATIONAL SHOWS

Here is a sampling of major national shows and events.

January

National Western Stock Show

International Finals Rodeo

American Grand Prix Association

National Jumper Championship

February

Florida Dressage Classic

March

Tampa Bay Classic

April

Junior & Amateur-Owner Invitational

Budweiser American Invitational

Rolex Three-Day Event

May

Kentucky Derby

Preakness Stakes

June

Belmont Stakes

Equitana USA

August

The Hambletonian (trotters)

September

Dressage at Devon

Little Brown Jug (pacers)

North American Endurance Championships

World Endurance Championships

U.S. Open Polo Championships

October

All-American Quarter Horse Congress

Arabian National Championships

Washington International Horse Show

November

AQHA World Championship Show

Breeders' Cup

December

National Finals Rodeo

GLOSSARY

aged: refers to any horse eight years and older

aids: means of communicating with the horse; the natural aids are the seat, legs, hands, and voice; artificial aids include spurs, whips, and other equipment

amateur: someone who is 18 years or older and is *not* paid for riding horses

blemish: any scar or acquired imperfection that is unsightly but does not affect a horse's soundness

body brush: an oval brush with short, soft bristles

breeches: specially designed riding pants, usually made from stretchy fabric. They fasten at the ankle and are meant to be worn with tall riding boots

bridle: the leather straps that hold the bit in the horse's mouth

canter: a comfortable three-beat gait

cantle: the back of the saddle

cavesson: the noseband of the bridle

colt: an entire (i.e., not gelded) male horse under four years of age

condition: physical fitness

conformation: the horse's physique; its build and shape

currycomb: a tool with several rows of teeth; metal currycombs are for cleaning brushes; rubber currycombs are for grooming the horse's coat

dandy brush: a wood-backed brush with long, stiff bristles, used to remove dirt and dried sweat from the horse's coat

diagonals: at the trot, the *up-down* rhythm to which the rider rises and sits; the rider should ride the outside diagonal, rising as the horse's outside foreleg comes forward

equestrian: a person who rides a horse

equitation: the art of riding horses

equitation classes: horse-show classes in which only the rider's skill is being judged

farrier: a blacksmith who shoes horses

filly: a female horse under four years of age

forehand: the part of the horse in front of the saddle; head, neck, shoulders, and forelegs

frog: the V-shaped rubbery part of the bottom of the horse's foot

gait: the pace at which a horse moves, such as walk, trot, canter, running walk, foxtrot, etc.

gelding: a castrated male horse of any age

girth: the strap that passes under the horse and holds the saddle in place

ground line: a pole placed on the ground in front of a jump, to help the horse estimate the height of the jump

hand: a four-inch unit of measurement, used when describing the height of horses

hay: dried grasses and legumes

head-shy: a horse that jerks its head away from an approaching hand

hoofpick: a small metal tool with a curved end, used to remove dirt and stones from a horse's hooves

hunter: a horse used as a field hunter or as a showring hunter

jodhpurs: specially-designed riding pants, usually made from stretchy fabric; they are longer than breeches, often have ankle cuffs, and are meant to be worn with paddock boots or riding sneakers

jumper: a horse that competes in jumping shows

leathers: stirrup leathers

mare: a female horse four years and older

near side: the horse's left side; horses are traditionally handled, led, and mounted from the left

off side: the horse's right side

paddock boots: short, lace-up riding boots to be worn with jodhpurs

passenger: a rider with no influence or effect on the horse

pommel: the raised arch at the front of the saddle

refusal: a horse that stops in front of a jump has "refused" the jump; his stop is called a refusal

riding boots: knee-high riding boots to be worn with breeches

riding sneakers: sneakers with a steel shank and low heel, designed for riding

run-out: a horse that avoids a jump by going past it instead of over it has "run out" at that jump; this action is called a run-out

school horse: a horse used in lessons at riding schools

schooling: practicing exercises and movements to improve the horse's and the rider's skills

snaffle: a bit that works by direct pressure on the horse's mouth; snaffles can be straight, or they can have one or two joints

sound: a horse that shows no sign of lameness

stallion: an entire (i.e., not gelded) male horse four years and older

tack: all the equipment that a riding horse wears; short for "tackle"

transitions: changes from one gait to another (e.g., walk to trot) or within a gait (e.g., working trot to medium trot)

trot: a rhythmic, bouncy two-beat gait

unsound: a horse that is lame or has some other health problem

walk: a rhythmic four-beat gait

withers: the bony area just in front of the saddle, between the horse's back and neck; horses are measured from the withers to the ground

INDEX

ABOUT THE AUTHOR

Jessica Jahiel, Ph.D. is an internationally known author, clinician, and lecturer. Certified by the American Riding Instructor Certification Program (ARICP) as an instructor of Dressage and Combined Training, Jessica teaches both children and adults at all levels. She has been closely associated with the United States Pony Clubs (USPC) for many years.

Jessica is the author of a critically-acclaimed and award-winning book, *Riding for the Rest of Us: A Practical Guide for Adult Riders* (Macmillan, 1996).

If you have Internet access, you can visit her sites on the World Wide Web. These include information about her writing and teaching (in-person clinics and video lessons), a column of book and tape reviews ("Horseman's Bookshelf"), and a freely downloadable book of games written for young riders. In her weekly electronic Q&A newsletter, *Horse-sense,* Jessica answers on-line questions about riding, training, tack, and horse management.

You can also hear Jessica answer horse-sense questions on Rick Lamb's radio program, *Horse Show.*

A popular lecturer, Jessica is a regularly featured speaker at Equitana USA and at the ARICP National Seminar. She is an active member of the speakers bureau of the American Medical Equestrian Association and the Russell Meerdink speakers bureau.

You can reach Jessica by mail at:

Jessica Jahiel
P.O. Box T
Savoy, IL 61874, USA
E-mail: jjahiel@prairienet.org
Web site: http://www.prairienet.org/jjahiel